FATHER JOHN GERARD: The Persecuted Priest

The Hides That Secured Him and the Tower That Could Not

Michael F. Morley

St Edward's Press Ltd

Formal Notes

Father John Gerard: The Persecuted Priest

First published in 2019 by
St Edward's Press Ltd

1st edition

ISBN 978-1-909650-09-1

Further copies of this book (with discounts on orders for more than one copy) may be ordered by emailing the publishers at info@stedwardspress.co.uk or via post to Hugh Williams, 20 Barra Close, Highworth, Wilts, SN67HX.

Cover Design by the author who says "Because of the nature of Fr Gerard's work, there is no authenticated portrait of him as, indeed, is the case for most, though not all, of his confreres. The image on the cover was therefore chosen as it bears a striking resemblance to contemporary descriptions of him and is based upon the portrait in the Kress Collection of an unknown young man, painted about 1550 by Francesco Salviati." Acknowledgements are also due to Simon French of Stable Studios, Highworth and Getty images.

Printed and bound in Great Britain by Marston Book Services Ltd, Oxfordshire

FATHER JOHN GERARD: The Persecuted Priest

Contents

About the Author

MICHAEL F. MORLEY

Michael Morley was born in East Sussex in 1947 and educated at St. Aloysius School in Oxford (now the Oxford Oratory) and at Salesian College, Cowley. His early interest in the past was sparked by a book given to him by his parents at Christmas, 1957, *"Robin Hood"* by Antonia Pakenham*, which began his lifelong love of real enquiry into medieval, then Tudor and Victorian history.

As a Catholic, Michael has naturally had a particular regard for the martyrs and saints of the sixteenth and seventeenth centuries; of the hardships endured by the faithful after the dissolution of the monasteries, and of the extraordinary courage of the Catholic priests and their lay helpers willing to suffer ruinous fines, torture and grisly death for the Faith in those penal times. This story of Father John Gerard and the genius of Blessed Nicholas Owen, the builder of so many crafty priest hides, manifests Michael's esteem for the heroes of those days and ends with a short reflective prayer for our own times....

Michael has recently retired as a teacher of History at St. Michael's School, Burghclere, and lives with his wife, Jane, in West Oxfordshire.

The author emerging from the priest hole at Huddington Court

* ...now the world-famous historian and novelist, Lady Antonia Fraser. Her early novel, *"Robin Hood"* is still in print and is recommended to any young person who may have a love of Merrie England, the Greenwood, chivalry, Our Blessed Lady, and a sense of justice and gallant deeds of derring-do!

Father John Gerard

Prologue

1564 is not a date that immediately impresses like 1066 or 1939. Nevertheless, it was a significant year which saw the deaths of Michelangelo and Jean Calvin and the births of Galileo, Christopher Marlowe and William Shakespeare. The first printed map of the British Isles was published by Mercator in his unique, albeit inaccurate "Projection", and Pieter Brueghel finished his paintings, "The Adoration of the Magi", (National Gallery) and "The Massacre of the Innocents", (The Royal Collection). The very first horse-drawn coach was brought to England from the Netherlands and the sweet potato arrived from the New World courtesy of the Elizabethan sea dog, Sir John Hawkins. Maximilian II was crowned Holy Roman Emperor and Sir Robert Dudley was appointed Earl of Leicester by Elizabeth I, "Gloriana" herself. The towering spire of old St. Paul's Cathedral in London was struck by a searing bolt from the blue and plunged with a fearful roar through the sanctuary roof and demolished the newly protestantised altar below, and John Gerard, the future heroic English missionary and hunted priest, was born at Bryn Hall in Lancashire. This year was not insignificant.

The year of 1570 was also fairly impressive; at least it was a busy one for Our Lord's representative on Earth, Pope Pius V. Not only did he promulgate the Bull "Quo Primum" after the Council of Trent made final, absolute and obligatory the Tridentine form of Mass according to the old Latin rite that still binds Catholics today, but this sainted pope also declared England's Queen Elizabeth excommunicated by her illegitimacy and released all her subjects from their allegiance to her. However, whilst understanding the Pontiff's move in wishing to make clear the position of English Catholics at this time, vis à vis the Church and the Faith, he inadvertently gave the Protestant authorities virtual carte blanche to accuse any Catholic - and particularly the hated priests - of treason against the monarch. Upon that excuse many hundreds of "papists" were subsequently hanged, drawn and quartered for simply trying to follow their Faith in those penal times.

Throughout all the upheavals of the early sixteenth century most of John Gerard's ancestors had remained true to the "Old Faith" never having taken the oath in recognition of Henry VIII's usurpation of the papal authority in 1535. When John was only five his father, Sir Thomas Gerard, was imprisoned for three years in the Tower of London for allegedly taking part in the plan to bring Mary Queen of Scots, the great granddaughter of Henry VII and the recognised rightful heir, to the throne of England. After her defeat at Langside in 1568, Mary was imprisoned by her cousin Elizabeth at Tutbury in Staffordshire, only two miles from where John was being cared for by relatives.

And so we begin Father Gerard's history. His own words, recorded in his autobiography of 1609, are written in *italics* throughout this narrative.

Chapter One
Iconoclasm and Destruction

To appreciate Father Gerard's story properly it may be necessary to present a little historical background. When Henry VIII ascended the throne in 1509 there was little to suggest the appalling consequences his reign would have upon the English nation and its Catholic faith. Until this time there had been no serious questioning of Church teaching, nor of that papal authority brought by St. Augustine to these islands almost a thousand years before. The Mass of Ages had been celebrated down the centuries in the awesome cathedrals and beautiful churches built for that purpose, most of which survive to this day although the majority have now, of course, been stripped of their former interior glories.

The backbone of Christendom in the Middle Ages was the monastic system and, by the turn of the sixteenth century, there were over five hundred monasteries in England and Wales. These powerhouses of prayer not only oversaw the spiritual welfare of the population, but they also looked after the temporal well-being and, to a large extent, the prosperity of the nation. Without these Christian institutions, mediaeval society, rich and poor, would have fallen apart.

Each monastery endeavoured to form a community which could look after itself to the point where no monk would need to leave its boundaries for anything outside except to preach and to bring the sacraments to the infirm and those who for any reason were unable to visit the abbey. Over time, as a monastery increased in size, it might come to form a quite substantial establishment covering many acres; some of the larger ones came almost to present the appearance of a small town within its boundary walls.

The monastic organisation was very strictly ordered and had a well-established routine. The daily round of prayers, the canonical eight offices, beginning with Matins at midnight and ending with Compline at nine in the evening, were recited every three hours, the monks being summoned to prayer by bells which would regularly have rung out over the fields and villages of mediaeval England. (See Page 70.)

The head of the monastery was the abbot who might also have been the lord of several manors or villages nearby and, as such, been able to provide work for many in the local population. His deputy was the prior; under him was the dean and then the monks themselves, each with his own allotted task within the community, perhaps farming, gardening, building or looking after the sick, cataloguing books or illuminating manuscripts and psalters. The priests among them provided Holy Mass and the sacraments for the people; they maintained schools and tutors, and undertook the education of novices brought to their doors. The monastery serviced medical care and hospitals for all in their area and gave food and shelter to passing travellers and pilgrims. Through the yearly round of ploughing, sowing, reaping, harvesting and milling flour, the monks were able to feed themselves as well as the surrounding community when times were hard. They also produced wine, ale and honey, not to mention meat, eggs, milk and bread; and, in their carefully cultivated ponds and streams they produced that most important Christian commodity for fast days and all Fridays...fish!

The practice of religion was so much a part of life that the whole population, from lords to commons, venerated the countless shrines set up in honour of God and His saints throughout the countryside, as one may still find in many places in Europe today. They worshipped Our Lord in the Blessed Sacrament and paid homage to His mother by parading her image through the streets on her feast days and reciting the rosary in public as they went about their daily business. Not for nothing was England known as the "Dowry of Mary".

All this was willingly accepted and common practice, the peaceful normality of life, until the coming of the great revolt now known as The Reformation. This revolution turned society upside down. It displaced

4

Christ, its former head and heart, by an entirely different world which was centred, not upon the will of God, but upon man's egocentric lust for the gratification of his own desires, which was more than amply demonstrated in England by its luxurious monarch, Henry VIII.

The young and handsome King Hal had earlier been welcomed by his English subjects with great joy after the oppression of his late father, the miserly tax-enthusiast Henry VII, whose tenuous claim to the throne had been strengthened by his military defeat of the last Plantagenet king, Richard III, at Bosworth Field in 1485. In the light of subsequent events it comes as quite a shock to recall the enthusiastic words of the thirty-one year old English lawyer, Thomas More, upon the coronation of Henry VIII: "This day is the end of our slavery, the fount of liberty; the end of sadness and the beginning of joy!" and who no doubt felt that his instincts had been correct when Henry later went on to write his "Treatise in Defence of the Seven Sacraments" against the apostate priest Martin Luther. Henry had consequently been awarded the title "Fidei Defensor" (Defender of the Faith) by a grateful Pope Leo X in 1521. This title was supposed to have been a one-off, bestowed upon Henry personally for his sterling rebuttal of Luther's pomps, but it has been falsely claimed by all British monarchs since then and "Fid. Def." or "F.D.", is still stamped upon the coins of the realm!

However, that Treatise, which was written in defence of the seven sacraments of the Church, had been published in 1521 but now, six years later, Henry demanded a divorce from his legitimate queen, Catherine of Aragon, by whom he had had no surviving male heir, in order to marry Anne Boleyn who was already carrying his bastard child, Elizabeth. The Holy Father could obviously not comply with this demand and so, in 1534, the king abolished the authority of the pope in England and passed a new law, the Act of Succession. Through Thomas Cranmer, his new and compliant Archbishop of Canterbury, Henry declared that the twenty-four years of marriage between himself and Catherine had always been invalid, she having been the wife of his dead brother Arthur, and it should therefore be annulled; obviously he had conveniently forgotten that the holy father had given his special dispensation to allow the marriage to take place all those years ago, and thus it was perfectly lawful and proper. However, Henry ordered that his new coupling with Anne Boleyn was to be recognised as his only true and legitimate marriage instead, and that any children resulting from their union were to be recognised by all as the only lawful heirs to the throne.

The Act of Supremacy was passed in the following year, 1535, making Henry "Supreme Head of the Church in England" and all the Church hierarchy, lords, commons and other nobles of the court were obliged to swear acceptance of the king's new title on pain of treason, which, of course, meant death by the hideous method of hanging, drawing and quartering! From now on Henry had declared himself to be Peter and ultimate spiritual authority in his own land. Thus in anger, lust, adultery and bigamy was born the Church of England.

Henry had had his greedy way and, thus emboldened, he rigorously set about slicing his realm from Rome. The dreadful story is well known: the execution of Catholics for denying the Act of Supremacy, as witnessed by Saints John Fisher, Bishop of Rochester and Sir Thomas More, former Chancellor of England, and the beginning of the suppression of the monasteries, were just the opening shots of the criminality that was to bring about the ruination of the Catholic faith in England under Henry VIII, Edward VI, Elizabeth I and James I.

This wanton destruction, carried out extremely efficiently by Henry's first minister, the vicious and obsequious Thomas Cromwell, included the dissolution of the monasteries and abbeys, nunneries, priories, hospitals, schools, hospices, orphanages and all the other institutions which had hitherto seen to the welfare of the poor, the sick and the hungry, the needy young and old, the crippled, the insane, the despised, the destitute and the dying simply because they were run and looked after by the Catholic Church whose visible head, under Christ, was the pope. Now, under Cromwell's direction, these institutions, along with their lands and all their goods and possessions, were confiscated by the commissioners of the king who enriched his own coffers by selling most of this stolen property to various court favourites and to others upon whom he could rely to support his megalomania and greed.

Next came the "Great Pillage". This consisted of the abolition and demolition of images, pictures and statues of saints, rood screens and ornaments of all kinds. Many thousands of priceless and beautiful works of art contained in ancient stained-glass windows were also deliberately shattered by flying stones to be lost forever.

Along with all this devastation went the wanton destruction of books and treasuries of illuminated manuscripts, many of them hundreds of years old, even then. Dozens of libraries, including that of the University of Oxford, laboriously and expensively collected, which included Anglo-Saxon chronicles and sagas, beautifully and lovingly written by hand, were shredded and burned in massive bonfires. Other treasures of gold and chalices of solid silver, precious stones and gems which had adorned altars or shrines, or been sewn onto exquisite and sumptuous Mass vestments beautifully crafted and blessed in service for the glory of God, all found their way into either Henry's avaricious hands or those of his accomplices.

The shrine of St. Thomas Becket, erected in Canterbury Cathedral, venerated since 1171 and made popular and famous through Geoffrey Chaucer's "Canterbury Tales", seems to have been a particular target for Henry's personal vindictiveness. Did he recall perhaps the odd coincidence of his predecessor namesake, Henry II, and the murder of another former chancellor of England, also called Thomas? The second Henry did at least try to make restitution for the murder of his former chancellor... but the eighth did not for his! In an unbelievably bizarre moment Henry VIII gave orders that Thomas Becket be summoned to appear in the king's court within thirty days to answer the charges laid against him by Henry II nearly four hundred years before! If Becket should not appear then Henry VIII would issue orders to Thomas Cromwell that this same shrine, Becket's body and all, should be utterly destroyed, broken up and looted of its treasures so that every vestige of its veneration and even of its exact location should be lost forever. All pilgrimages, not just those to Canterbury "the holy blessed martyr for to seek" (Chaucer), were then abolished and outlawed in perpetuity. But to the apparent astonishment of all, Thomas Becket did not appear to answer any charges and so the Tudor's orders were enthusiastically carried out!

So what happened to these religious foundations, their revenues and their lands? What happened to the clergy? It should be remembered that, up until 1536, all monasteries, religious properties, their lands and estates had been owned by the Church and paid for by the people through their tithes, or through the patronage of noble families. This privilege had always been accepted and protected by the monarchs of England; indeed, they had all taken oaths to do so. Some may have had their disputes, but none had actually denied the authority of the Church and all had acknowledged that their own jurisdiction had come through the grace of God manifested and upheld by the Vicar of Christ; hence the Divine Right of Kings upon which they all insisted. Church and State were meant to rule together under the authority of God and even King John had eventually come to acknowledge that fact! But, through the rage of Henry VIII, the clergy was depleted and beggared, and large numbers were slaughtered. Many fled to the Continent or embraced the new religion and accepted small pensions through fear; but many did not. After hanging, drawing and quartering in 1539, various parts of Abbot Richard Whiting were nailed to the door of his abbey at Glastonbury.

The roofs of these great buildings had the lead stripped from them and the timbers carted off to be used in other buildings or in the construction of ships and weaponry. Without this protection the walls were easily penetrated by the weather and the great edifices began to crumble and fall apart, the local manorial lords then using the stones from these convenient "quarries" to expand their own towns and villages. Today there is nothing left at all to remind us of the location of so many of these wonderful buildings erected "ad majorem Dei gloriam" ("to the greater glory of God".) For instance, the once great Benedictine Abbey of Eynsham, built upon the banks of the Thames six miles west of Oxford, where kings had formerly convoked meetings of the great and good of Church and State, and where once the famous St. Hugh of Lincoln was abbot, was dissolved in December 1539 and has, quite literally, like the temple of Jerusalem, not one stone left upon another!

It is estimated that eventually at least eight hundred and fifty monasteries and religious houses in England and Wales were looted and destroyed and that over two thousand more church properties and institutions, including those under the patronage of a number of great and powerful families, such as the de Veres in Essex, did not escape attention.

All the properties belonging to the four Orders of Friars (Augustinians, Carmelites, Dominicans and Franciscans), free chapels, chantries, churches and convents including the ancient and most venerated shrine of Our Lady of Walsingham in Norfolk, founded in 1061, were also plundered, variously disposed of and scattered. Suddenly enriched beyond the dreams of avarice none of the new beneficiaries, supporters of the grasping king and traitors to their Church, could ever have been expected to return to their former religion…. they might, after all, have been required at the same time to return their ill-gotten gains and this was one reason why Mary Tudor was unable later to restore the country to Catholicism during her five-year reign; support for that idea was not forthcoming.

In short, the Catholic faith was being forced out of the country by theft and persecution, leaving the population terrified, spiritually bereft and confused. Henry VIII was the first monarch who had dared to lay profane hands upon the sacred and to deny Christ's right to rule society through His Church. He broke with a thousand years of tradition hitherto carefully and assiduously guarded by most of his predecessors, and from that devastation neither England nor Christendom has ever recovered.

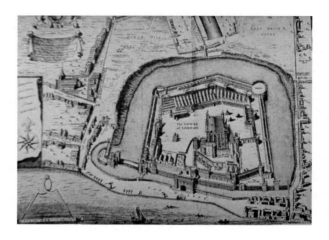

The Tower of London 1597 See enlarged detail below

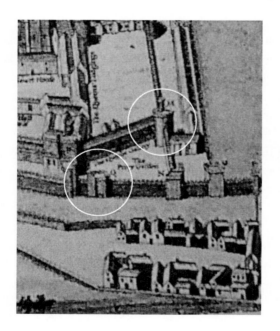

The Salt Tower – circled above.

The Cradle Tower – circled below.

← The Moat

← The River Thames

Chapter Two
Vocation and Fervour

This, then, had been the bloody rejection of the Catholic Church by the king and the enforced installation, upon an unwilling people, of the wholly novel Protestant religion "as by law established". So, when John Gerard was sent to Exeter College, Oxford in December, 1575, in high hopes of a classical education, he found his stay there cut short for *"...at Easter (1576) the heretics sought to force us to attend their worship and to partake of their counterfeit sacrament"*. He therefore continued his schooling with tutors at home before moving to Cardinal Allen's English College at Douai in the Spanish Netherlands and afterwards, when the college had been expelled from there, at the University of Rheims, where he studied humanities and scripture. Three years later he attended Clermont College in Paris to further his studies and to experience something of the Jesuit life. Whilst there he met Father Persons who advised him to return home and to put his affairs in order before pursuing a religious career - for John Gerard had determined to join the Society of Jesus.

The now nineteen-year-old Gerard, keen to pursue a priestly vocation, had hoped to slip back into England unnoticed but contrary winds forced his boat into Dover where customs officials arrested him and dispatched him to London. Despite honestly declaring himself a Catholic he was not imprisoned but was sent to be detained by his uncle, a Protestant, who attempted, but failed, to pervert his nephew's mind. Being so obdurate John was eventually sent to the Marshalsea prison where, he writes, *"...I found numbers of Catholics and some priests awaiting judgement and death with the greatest joy!"*

These Catholic prisoners had found ways to acquire books and missals, altar plate and vestments and were thus able secretly to celebrate Mass. But eventually the authorities got wind of the situation, a search was made and so much "massing stuff" was retrieved from hiding holes that it filled a whole cart. However, friends on the outside were able to smuggle in replacement items so that normal Catholic life on the inside of the prison was quickly and quietly restored!

Gerard remained in the Marshalsea for over a year and, when he was released on parole at Easter, 1585, he seized the opportunity gratefully to escape to the Continent by way of a sympathetic boatman, and eventually he arrived at the English College in Rome.

John Gerard was ordained three years later and, with his good friend, Edward Oldcorne, was admitted by the Father General, Claudius Acquaviva, into the Society of Jesus on the feast of the Assumption, 1588. This was the year of the Spanish Armada, the unsubtle and abortive attempt by King Philip II of Spain to invade and return England to the Catholic Faith. This proved to be a very unwise move on the part of the Spanish king as it served only to enrage the English, both Protestant and not a few Catholics also, whose righteous indignation was aroused by the idea of foreign military intervention in the affairs of their sovereign country! This would not help the mission of the incoming priests but, nothing daunted, Father Gerard, in the company of Father Oldcorne, both in disguise, made a clandestine landing on the remote Norfolk coast one bleak and rainy night in November that year. They were determined, gently and quietly, to succeed where King Philip had failed in his blunt fashion to return the succour of the Mass and the blessed sacraments to persecuted Catholics in England.

All the English Jesuits returning from the Continent to their homeland had, of course, been very well-warned of the dangers they would be facing at every turn. Every one of them, for instance, knew the story of Edmund Campion, the Protestant Oxford academic who had once found favour with Queen Elizabeth for his debating skills and been spoken of as a future Archbishop of Canterbury in the new Tudor order…had he played his cards right! In due course, however, having become convinced of the rightness and validity of Catholicism, he had gone to study at the English College in Douai in the Netherlands and was finally ordained priest in 1578. Campion had then returned to his native country in company with his confrere, Robert Persons, the first two founding priests of the Jesuit mission in England, intent upon bringing the Faith to wretched souls left abandoned by the new "reforms". But although Persons had survived and eventually died a peaceful death in Rome, Campion had been betrayed, captured, tortured and stretched three times on the rack, before finally being brought to trial. Even his great and noted gifts of eloquence and patience could not prevail against a national regime intent upon the destruction of Catholic priests within its jurisdiction and so, in the company of two other young Jesuits, Alexander Briant and Ralph Sherwin, Edmund Campion had been convicted of high treason and hanged, drawn and quartered at Tyburn in 1581.

But even knowing all this and appreciating the martyrdom that might await them, large numbers of such brave men were determined to follow Campion's example, Fathers Gerard and Oldcorne among them, and so, having spent their first dark and soaking hours in a dripping wood, the two priests split up and made their various ways to London. Gerard, pretending to be a falconer who had lost his hawk, was able to proceed slowly but safely across country to Norwich without attracting undue attention. He was only once stopped briefly and questioned by government officials in Horsham St. Faith keeping a lookout for Catholic priests, spies and other "traitors likely to cause harm to the queen's person or peace", but they were apparently satisfied by his answers and allowed him the freedom to continue the search for his bird!

Once he reached Norwich, Gerard made the acquaintance of Edward Yelverton, a Catholic gentleman who gave him shelter for several days in his own house. Having procured a horse through the good offices of this gentleman, the priest then travelled on to London without mishap, where he carefully sought out and made himself known to his new superior, Father Henry Garnet.

Including the superior there were just five Jesuit priests in England at this time (1588), the others being Edmund Weston, Robert Southwell, Edward Oldcorne and, of course, John Gerard himself, but only four were now gathered in London, Weston having already been caught and incarcerated in Wisbech in the Cambridgeshire Fenland. Garnet and Southwell were able to brief the two newcomers and apprise them of the safest methods of undertaking their priestly mission while keeping themselves free of imprisonment, torture or worse. They were informed of the most trustworthy men and women who were prepared to lose everything in offering the priests board and shelter, sometimes in the most imaginative of hiding places when the pursuivants came too close. This was particularly the lot of John Gerard, as we shall see.

By Christmas this year the priests had dispersed into East Anglia and parts of the Midlands, and so it was that there now appeared at Grimston in Norfolk a young gentleman of moderate means, "tall and well-set with a dark complexion, his beard close, saving little mustachoes and a little tuft under his lower lip" (part of a "wanted" description of John Gerard circulated at the time of the Gunpowder Plot in 1605), carrying a gilded rapier and a silver dagger, apparently a dear and old friend of Edward Yelverton, who had come to stay as a guest in his house. In this disguise and using various aliases at different times during his long and eventful mission (such as, Mister Brooke or Palmer or Staunton), Father Gerard was able to move about the countryside avoiding the suspicion of those who would harbour ill-will towards him and, thereby, also protecting those friends who were well aware of his true identity and business. This kind of subterfuge had to be the resort of all the priests and for a long time it worked well for Gerard.

During the ensuing months he was pleased to be able to *"gain over and convert many to the Church and to steady many tottering souls in their allegiance, and I heard many general confessions"*. He said Mass and administered the sacraments to Catholics who sometimes had not received them for decades. He brought solace to the sick and the comfort of the Church to all those who must almost have despaired of ever seeing a priest again, and he was also instrumental in sending a number of young men to the Continent to try their vocations.

After a while, though, he began to feel that he was becoming rather too well known in those parts to the possible detriment of everyone's safety, and so he moved his lodgings twice more to keep the authorities off his scent. These first three years in England had been very productive and relatively uneventful for Father Gerard, but all this was about to change.

Chapter Three
Concealment and Search

It had been the custom of the priests, who were now beginning to grow in number, to meet together with their superior twice a year to render an account of their doings and to renew their vows, and so, in October 1591, they all gathered with Father Garnet at Baddesley Clinton in Warwickshire, a large and moated stone house dating from the 13th century and owned by the Catholic Henry Ferrers. This gentleman was an antiquary and expert in his knowledge of heraldry, who was usually in debt and who, whilst presently away on business in London, had rented his manor house to Anne Vaux, a twenty-nine year old spinster and family friend. This young lady had devoted her life to the noble but extremely dangerous vocation of harbouring Catholic priests from the Protestant authorities who were hunting them down for imprisonment, expulsion or execution.

Suddenly, one morning at five o'clock, as Father Southwell was beginning Mass, there came a thunderous pounding at the great gate. A posse of pursuivants, with weapons drawn, had crossed the moat and were loudly demanding admittance. An exceptionally courageous manservant was refusing them entry claiming that the lady of the house, Miss Anne Vaux, was still abed but that he would ask her to be roused to ascertain what their business might be! The time thus gained was used to strip the altar and stow away all the vestments and paraphernalia vital for the celebration of Mass, along with the priests' baggage, boots and spurs. Their recently vacated mattresses were turned cold-side up in case inquisitive hands might detect the warmth of persons as yet unaccounted for in the house.

No fewer than seven priests and three laymen helpers lowered themselves down from the first-floor chapel through a hollowed drop within the thickness of the great stone wall, past the kitchen beneath and into a long culvert below ground and moat level. There they stood with their feet in water, shivering in mute fear for what must have seemed an age while the ruffians above rampaged through the house searching every obvious nook and cranny for their prey. However, the desperate priests were fortunate that day for this was a brief investigation only, a cursory probing lasting but four hours and, although wet and uncomfortable, the Baddesley Clinton hide was relatively large.

In these seemingly never-ending penal years searches could last many days, sometimes even up to a fortnight, while the hapless, hunted priests must survive in calm dumbness, half scared out of their wits within the silent claustrophobic fabric of massive mediaeval houses, often drenched in their own sweat in summer or nearly frozen to death in winter, mostly without food or water and, although some were provided with no more than a bucket of earth, nearly all were without toilet facilities of any kind. The hides that sheltered them were usually tiny, some so cramped that the unfortunate fugitive could barely sit down, let alone recline to rest. They would hardly dare to draw breath lest a catch in the throat should elicit a cough for, whilst hidden away, they had to remain as motionless as possible.

Of course, not every search was commotion and violence all the time. More than one tactic might be employed, and the frightened man was not to know whether a pursuer at dusk might be creeping quietly around the room nearby listening intently for any sound or rustle as the priest moved slightly, perhaps even trying to stifle a cry of agony in relieving a sudden excruciating cramp in the leg. They had always to be on their guard so as not to arouse the suspicion of an enemy, possibly waiting patiently, stock-still and soundlessly, in the shadows at the end of a passage, to detect the slightest hint of movement which would have betrayed the presence of a hidden papist. These hunted priests knew that silence was of the essence and they must surely have been aware even of their own pounding heartbeats. Although exhausted, sleep would have been virtually impossible as they knew some involuntary disturbance, a sneeze or a snore, could alert a pursuer who might be only inches away beyond the wooden panelling. Some jittery brute could easily pierce a hide wall with a probing pike, serious injury could be inflicted, and a discovered priest hauled off triumphantly in chains to the butcher's block.

It was most unlikely that there would have been a window in such a hole, and so it was always night in these lonely places of concealment. It would have been very easy to become disorientated and to lose track of the passing of day and night as the fear-filled hours ticked endlessly by. In these cramped conditions the foul air and darkness could never be alleviated by the comfort and warmth of a candle – the risk was just too great. A tell-tale chink of light might be seen beyond in a dark room through some crack in the plaster or mortar, through a floorboard, a stairway or a bookcase or even through a break in a brick; and, in the snuffing of a candle, who could mistake that distinctive scent? Certainly not a seasoned priest-hunter. Yet, through the providence of God, very many lives were spared, or at least lengthened, because of these artful constructions, the awful conditions notwithstanding.

And so it was at Baddesley Clinton. The search discovered no priests and the bullies reluctantly gave up in disgust, but not before they had forced payment from the owners of the house for the time spent in fruitless pursuit! As Gerard indignantly declared, *"So pitiful is the lot of the Catholics that those who come with a warrant to annoy them in this or in any other way, have to be paid for so doing by the suffering party instead of by the authorities who actually send them!"* The good Fathers had at least escaped capture this time and so they were *"…summoned out of the den, not one, but many Daniels!"*, and the following day they made good their escape, each returning to his own county. John Gerard had indeed avoided capture but, for the first time since his arrival as a priest in England, he had had a foretaste of the mortal danger that was to threaten him from this moment on.

––––––––––––––––––––

During that winter of 1591/92, John Gerard gratefully took up residence at the manor of Broad Oaks, commonly known as Braddocks, a large and lovely brick-built manor house set in its own estate in Essex, at the insistent invitation of its owner, Mr. William Wiseman. This gentleman was, amongst other things, a lawyer for members of Parliament which inevitably meant that his business would take him away for long periods of time to London leaving his wife, Jane, to look after the estate. Gerard was made to feel very welcome and was able to continue his priestly mission from Braddocks for some time but, unbeknown to him or to his hosts, one of the servants was about to wreak havoc upon the household.

Although not a Catholic, John Frank was loved and trusted by his employers and was thus privy to most of what went on in the house. He was not absolutely certain that the guest to whom his master gave so much deference was indeed a priest, but he did voice his suspicions to the authorities. Thus, the first order to search the Wiseman estate went out at Christmas, 1593, and the pursuivants came down upon the house of William Wiseman's mother at Northend on the feast of St. Stephen, 26th December. Gerard was visiting the old lady at the time and it appears probable that Frank had notified the authorities of the fact. But, after a half-hearted search which failed to find the priest, (who was hidden in a cramped chamber constructed within a chimney), the relieved members of the conscripted posse were happily dismissed to return to their homes to continue their interrupted Christmas celebrations with their families.

John Frank was, however, persistent in his suspicions of Gerard and this resulted in the arrest and imprisonment of William Wiseman shortly before Easter in the Counter prison in London. A second order then went out to the magistrates of Essex charging them to search Braddocks forthwith.

On Easter Monday, April 1st, 1594, just before dawn, the pursuivants crept up upon the manor, which was already preparing for Mass, and battered at the main door. The traitor, no doubt with a wink to the bailiffs, made a great pretence of slowing their entrance but soon the search party spread out through the house intent upon rooting out their quarry. Mrs. Jane Wiseman pushed a jar of quince jelly and a couple of biscuits into his hands and bundled Gerard into the hiding place adjacent to the chapel in the roof and he literally disappeared into the fabric of the building without a trace.

For the next two days the vandals ransacked the house, smashing down doors, ripping plaster off walls, crowbarring through wooden panels and stabbing with swords into dark crevices for the hated priest. *"They measured the walls with long rods so that if they did not tally they might pierce the part not accounted for. They sounded the walls and all the floors to discover and break into any hollow places there might be",* wrote Gerard; but they found nothing and the officers, angrily deciding that their bird must already have flown, began their journey back to London with the mistress and Catholic servants of the house, intending to have them, at least, imprisoned.

The captive Mrs. Wiseman, pleased at least to have the destructive search concluded at last, quietly, but yet unwittingly, instructed the apparently still faithful John Frank to call out to Gerard when they had left, that it was safe for him to emerge from his refuge. Although he was not privy to the whereabouts of the hide Frank immediately informed the bailiffs that the man they were hunting was almost certainly still in the house. Back they came to renew their efforts more diligently than before!

The hiding place in which Father Gerard was presently concealed needs description. It was most cunningly designed and constructed by one of the Jesuits' most faithful lay brothers and servants of the Catholic cause known generally to his contemporary friends as "Little John". He is better known to us as Nicholas Owen. He was lame, apparently having suffered as a lad from a kick by a horse, and not very tall; but he had phenomenal strength. His stature may not have been remarkable, but his achievements are astonishing and unsurpassed. His reputation as a builder of priest holes is now legendary although, of course, the nature of his work and even his very existence had to remain secret and undetected in his lifetime. He was a carpenter and mason from Oxford whose extraordinarily inventive mind produced the most ingenious hiding places in a great number of Catholic houses across England; it is thought that even today there are still a number of his hides that remain undetected. Who knows how many lives were saved by his skilful ingenuity? The great man was eventually captured and died under torture in the Tower of London on March 2nd, 1606, but without giving up the smallest secret of his work.

On the second floor of the north wing of Braddocks Manor, and running under the roof space, was a long room converted by the Wisemans into a private chapel which contained a fireplace set within one of the side walls. In the previous year (1593) Nicholas Owen, whilst on a visit to the manor at the invitation of Father Gerard, had noticed this feature and imagined that it could have some potential for his ability as a hide builder, and so he began to take soundings with his hammer. He discovered it would be possible to quarry out a narrow chamber within the thick wall upon which the fireplace was constructed, underneath the hearth itself and off-set slightly to the left, which could be made large enough and deep enough to conceal a man. The entrance to this chamber would be effected from the chapel under a partly false hearth floor composed of a wood base and bricks which could be slid back into position once the fugitive had scrambled down into the hide beneath. (See diagram on Page 73.) Kindling and firewood would then be laid in the fireplace to complete the deception although the hearth itself would not now be strong enough to bear the weight and heat of a fire, having been necessarily weakened by the hollowed-out cavity below.

So here languished the unfortunate priest, in possession only of the quince jelly and biscuits, but now in the third day of his confinement beneath this fireplace, in a hole not much larger than a brick-built tomb. I think we should let Gerard, in his matter-of- fact manner, calmly describe what happened next, based upon his autobiography.

He writes, "*The pursuivants returned early in the morning and renewed their search. They measured and sounded everywhere, much more carefully than before, in order to find out some hollow place. But they found nothing whatever during the whole of the third day. So they set guards in all the rooms about to watch all night lest I should escape. I heard from my hiding place the password which the captain of the band gave to his soldiers, and I might have escaped by using it were it not that they would have seen me issuing from my retreat: for there were two on guard in the chapel where I got into my hiding place.*

"But mark the wonderful providence of God! Here was I in my hiding place. The way I got into it was by taking up the floor, made of wood and bricks, under the fireplace. The place was so constructed that a fire could not be lit in it without damaging the house; though we made a point of keeping wood there as if it were meant for a fire. Well, the men on the

night watch lit a fire in this very grate and began chatting together very close to it!

"Soon the bricks, which had not bricks but wood beneath them, got loose and nearly fell out of their places as the wood gave way. On noticing this and probing the fire with a stick, they found that the bottom was made of wood, whereupon they remarked that this was something curious. I thought that they were going there and then to break open the place and enter; but they made up their minds at last to put off further examination till next day.

"Meanwhile, I besought the Lord earnestly that, if it were for the glory of His Name, I might not be taken in that house and so endanger my entertainers; nor in any other house where others would share my disaster. My prayer was heard and I was preserved in that house in a most wonderful manner.

"Next morning, therefore, they renewed the search most carefully, everywhere except in the top chamber which served as a chapel, and in which the two watchmen had made a fire over my head and had noticed the strange make of the grate. God had blotted out of their memory all remembrance of the thing. Nay, none of the searchers entered the place the whole day, though it was the one most open to suspicion and if they had entered, they would have found me without any search; rather, I should say, they would have seen me, for the fire had burned a great hole in my hiding place and, had I not got a little out of the way, the hot embers would have fallen upon me.

"The searchers, forgetting or not caring about this room, busied themselves in ransacking the rooms below. They did indeed find a little hidden place there, but the shouts of joy soon turned to grief when they discovered I was not within. Frank, the traitor, must have found his elation fast turned to desolation in his disappointment.

"They stuck to their purpose, however, and set a man to work near the ceiling under the chapel floor, close to where I was. They worked away from me all around the room below till they came again to the very place

where I lay, and there they lost heart and gave up the search. God, who set bounds to the sea, said also to their dogged obstinacy, 'Thus far shalt thou go and no further'.

"Seeing that their toil availed them nought, they thought that I had escaped somehow and so they went away at the end of four days, leaving the mistress and her servants free. The yet undiscovered traitor stayed after the searchers were gone. As soon as the doors of the house were made fast Mrs. Wiseman came to call me from what would have been my grave had the search continued any longer. For I was all wasted and weakened, as well with hunger as with want of sleep and with having to sit so long in such a narrow place. The mistress of the house, too, had eaten nothing whatever during the whole time, not only to share my distress but chiefly to draw down the mercy of God on me, herself and her family, by this fasting and prayer."

The whole household rejoiced to find Father Gerard so miraculously preserved. Even Frank made a pretence of joy, but we can imagine the inner turmoil that must have distracted him: would he be rejected as unreliable by his real friends? Would he be discovered by those he sought to betray and so lose his home and his livelihood? Inwardly he must have uttered a frightened and astonished oath to behold a pale and unshaven Gerard staggering, unsteadily but safe, down to the great kitchen.

Two days later, fearing for everyone's safety, the priest reluctantly left Braddocks where he had been so happy, and soon arrived again in London to reassure his anxious friends that he was indeed unharmed and eager to renew his mission. He acquired lodgings and met up once more with Nicholas Owen and, as he writes now in his autobiography, *"It was God's will that my hour should then come"*.

Chapter Four
Capture and Torture

The traitor, John Frank, had completely eluded all suspicion and was, incredibly, still so trusted as to become letter bearer between the Wiseman family and others of their friends. He therefore had confidential information regarding the whereabouts of prominent persons and much other secret knowledge of Catholic affairs, and so he sought the chance to redeem his recent failure in the eyes of the State authorities.

One evening in late April 1594, he brought a letter addressed to Gerard in his new London lodgings, but instead of returning the reply entrusted to him, this latter-day Judas could hardly wait to betray the priest who had so recently caused him so much grief and embarrassment. Overtaken by thoughts of revenge he hurried to inform the local magistrate where this fugitive could be found and so it was that, as Father Gerard and Little John were preparing quietly to settle down for the night, the priest-hunters came crashing through their door. The two men were taken at sword-point and Gerard was dragged off to one of the commissioners' houses to face a dangerous investigation.

It was obvious the authorities knew they had their man and Gerard realised there was no point in dissembling.

"Are you a priest?".
"Yes".

"Who sent you into England?".
"My religious superiors".

"To what end?".
"To bring back stray souls to their Creator".

"How long have you been here?".
"About six years".

"Where did you land and who has given you shelter?".

"This I cannot answer in good conscience, for I may bring misfortune upon innocent heads".

"You were sent for sedition against the queen and you will answer, if not by goodwill then by force".

"No", Gerard replied, *"I hope not. You must accept my answers as true and that I may not disclose all you demand".*

The annoyed magistrate, Richard Young, then committed his captive to the small Counter prison in the noisome poultry market area, described by Father Garnet as "a very evil prison and without comfort". Gerard was forced into a low room which he had to enter stooped, and on his knees, and which was situated next to the privy used by all the nearby prisoners. Its foul stench often kept him awake and, because his window could not be closed, the rain frequently blew in and soaked his bed.

After four days in this stinking hole Gerard was called forth for a second examination by the magistrate and another man. This person was Richard Topcliffe, possibly the most feared and loathed by Catholics of all the queen's officials, the current tormentor and eventual destroyer of Robert Southwell, another famously heroic Jesuit priest and one of Gerard's companions.

"This creature from Hell (Topcliffe) *had been raised up by God to test the merits of His saints. Malignant, obscene and with an enormous brutality… he was chief pursuivant, leading raids with his own private army, prison governor and torturer, assistant prosecutor at trials and supervisor of the disembowellings"*, writes Gerard. He was also a rapist and a perjurer and bore the unique title of "Queen's Servant". However, not even this depraved villain could make Gerard give any further information and so he was sent back to his disgusting dungeon but now, on Topcliffe's order, with his legs locked in weighty irons. Father Gerard recalls that he welcomed these irons as something more to endure for Our Blessed Lord.

Meanwhile, Nicholas Owen and, later, Father Gerard's servant, Richard Fulwood who had also been betrayed by Frank, were put to the cruellest torture and Gerard describes how *"...they were strung up for three hours together, having their arms fixed into iron rings and their bodies hanging in the air; a torture which causes frightful pain and intolerable extension of the sinews."* But neither of them surrendered any information and no address or family name was ever betrayed; and none other of Gerard's acquaintance came forward to say they knew him. Richard Fulwood managed to escape soon after and Nicholas Owen was bought out of prison by some Catholic acquaintances, the authorities having, at that time, no understanding of the incalculable worth of this little man!

After further fruitless questionings, Young, the magistrate, gave up in frustration but, with the offer of a little pecuniary reward by Gerard's friends, agreed to transfer the priest to the Clink.

This prison was a definite improvement upon the last. There were many of the faithful there who had established a great Catholic infrastructure and he was unexpectedly able to resume his priestly mission. It was not the same, of course, for he had not the liberty to roam the shires nor to make new friends nor to visit old, which naturally vexed him, but at least he could not now suddenly be arrested and risk the lives of other helpful recusants. And, if he did not have that larger and freer congregation, he did, at least, have this smaller but captive one!

He soon realised that the regime in this place, whilst appearing outwardly strict, had become somewhat susceptible to a little corruption by the inmates and their friends on the outside, and many had even contrived to make copies of their cell keys. Father Gerard was thus able in prison to hear confessions and to preach the Spiritual Exercises of Saint Ignatius which prompted many of the incarcerated back to the Faith. But what brought him most joy was in finding that, if he rose earlier in the morning than his late-rising warder, he was actually able to celebrate Mass for the faithful in another part of the gaol. It was here that he met John Lillie *"...whom God's providence had shut up there for his own good and mine"*, who became one of his truest and most dependable friends during these years of imprisonment. Of this period he wrote that, although conditions were obviously far from ideal, he would, given the circumstances, have been pleased to spend the rest of his life working even within this modicum of freedom!

Nevertheless, he was closely interrogated by the authorities on three or more separate occasions regarding his mission. The queen's inquisitors tried to get him to admit that he was planning, with others, a rebellion against her; that he would support an outside invasion of England if it were sanctioned by the pope; that he had encouraged others to become priests and therefore he and they would be rebellious subjects of the monarch, and that he fostered the preposterous and seditious notion that only the pope could be the spiritual head of the church in England, thereby rejecting her Majesty Queen Elizabeth's own true claim. That way lay treason! Gerard, however, countered all these accusations by explaining that, as a priest, he was forbidden by his superiors to dabble in politics and was only in England on a commission to reconcile souls to God and, through the sacraments, to bring them to Heaven.

As the authorities had no proof to support their allegations, they could not proceed in law against him and so, in their anger and disappointment, they sent him to the Tower of London for further questioning under torture. He was transferred to this fortress, this prison of previous Catholic martyrs, in April, 1597.

Upon being handed over to the King's Lieutenant, Gerard was marched off to the Salt Tower and given over into the custody of one Master Bennet, the gaoler there, who took him up to the cell where he spent his first night upon a little straw on the stone floor. He commended himself to God and the Blessed Virgin, to his patron saints and his Guardian Angel and, considering the circumstances and the far from certain future, he remembers that he slept quite well that night.

At dawn his natural apprehension returned and, in this dim light of early day, he set about examining his new prison. Imagine his excited delight when he unexpectedly came upon the name of Henry Walpole carved neatly into one of the stone walls. This blessed Father had also written in chalk on the wall nearby, the name of God in Latin, Greek and Hebrew, under that the name of Jesus and under that again the name of Mary, Mother of God. Lastly, he had written the names of the Cherubim and Seraphim and listed the nine choirs of angels. Father Gerard knew that this holy man had been hanged, drawn and quartered for his priesthood exactly two years before. Unfortunately, Father Walpole had been captured only twenty-four hours after landing on the Yorkshire coast and had been executed in York after enduring more than three lonely years in captivity and repeated torture in the Tower of London.

Unbeknown to them both, there was an interesting coincidence connecting these two priests, apart from their both being Jesuits, which came to light only much later. It appears they were heroes to each other. Having been ordained in Paris, Father Walpole had always wanted to return to England to bring back the Faith to his desperate countrymen but, for so long, to his great regret, he was unable to gain that permission from his superiors who sent him instead to teach in the English seminaries in Flanders and Spain. But, according to his biographers, he was heard very often to exclaim, "Oh, that John Gerard doth much good in England! Why, then, not I?" So Gerard had inspired Walpole by his missionary life in their homeland and now Walpole was inspiring Gerard by his imprisonment and death!

Father Gerard's joyful consolation in finding himself in the martyr's dungeon was short-lived, for he was presently ordered into the prison chamber above in the same tower. He tried to explain to Bennet why he did not wish to be removed and that unhappy man did seem to understand but answered that he was only obeying orders! But, slightly against the rules, he did agree to allow his prisoner to visit Walpole's cell often to pray. The warder also offered to fetch any basic necessities from Gerard's friends, to which offer he replied that he had no friends, so as not to implicate those still at liberty, except those in the Clink, his former prison. However, he did mention that those acquaintances would gladly donate anything he needed and, indeed, upon Gerard's request, they supplied him with a bed and some clothing, and Bennet, acting as go-between, was paid for his services.

The following day Gerard was taken to face the Lord's Commissioners and the Attorney General, Sir Edward Coke. They demanded that he confess to various charges that would have admitted treason against the queen and the State which, through his subversive activity, would endanger the realm. They asserted that he had received letters from overseas containing instructions for sedition which he had since delivered to his superior, Henry Garnet. What did these letters contain? Where was Garnet hiding now? Father Gerard gave the answer he had given before: his cause in England was only to have the opportunity to save souls. This was unsatisfactory and William Wade, Secretary of the Privy Council, was furious.

"Where is Garnet?", he shouted. "He is an enemy of the State".

"Not so. He is no enemy of the State. But, even if I did know his whereabouts, I would not tell you".

"But you shall tell us before we leave this place", was the angry reply and Wade produced a duly signed warrant to put Gerard to the torture.

"By the help of God I will never do what is against Him, against justice and against the Catholic faith. You have me in your power; do what God permits you, for you certainly cannot go beyond. I do not fear what you can do to me since all of us are in God's hands".

So saying, Gerard was led away to an underground chamber lit only by candles, but it was enough to show him many instruments of torture; enough to put such fear into a man that the mere sight of them might be enough to incite him to betray his friends and his faith. Father Gerard fell to his knees imploring God's help to give him strength enough to endure whatever evil may be about to fall upon him, but he was violently hauled to his feet by being suddenly tugged upright by the manacles they had attached to his wrists. They pulled his arms above his head and, with an iron bar, fastened them to two heavy iron rings set into a pillar. Being of taller stature than most, (he was known affectionately by some of his friends as "Long John"), his tormentors found they could not stretch his whole length off the ground but, nothing daunted, they sent for Hodge, a labourer employed by the Tower, to dig away the earth beneath his feet until his whole weight was suspended in the air by his hands. Being such a strong man Gerard was not in too much discomfort to begin with, but very soon he experienced the most excruciating pain in his chest and stomach and began to feel his flesh swelling over the iron bars that held his wrists. He thought that blood was being forced through the tips of his fingers, the pressure was so great.

He began to pray as the men around exhorted him to confess that his mission in England was more politically subversive than spiritual and to give them the information they wanted. He was consoled by God's assurance, given to all men, that he would not be tested beyond his endurance but, anyway, had he not always longed to give his life for his Saviour? This thought seemed to make the pain more bearable.

Wade and his cronies gave up in disgust and left Gerard in the chamber with four men to supervise his torture. He kept repeating the names of Jesus and Mary and, after two hours of this cruelty, he lost consciousness. The men put some steps under his feet to support him and threw water over him until he revived and then, when Gerard began to pray again, they moved them away leaving him suspended once more. Over the next four hours he fainted nine more times and the revival procedure was repeated again and again.

A little before five o'clock Wade returned and asked whether Gerard was now disposed to talk to the Council or, at least, to Secretary Cecil?

"I have nothing to say to either of you", Gerard gasped, *"beyond what I have said already"*.

"Hang there, then, till you rot!", and Wade stormed off in a rage.

Shortly after, Gerard was released from the manacles but, although his legs were unharmed, he could barely stand. Bennet, his gaoler was stunned to see his charge brought back in such a pitiful condition and sympathetically helped him return to his cell where he lit a fire and brought him some food. He then saw him to bed where the priest lay quietly all night.

The next morning, before breakfast, Gerard was again brought before William Wade who vowed that the queen herself and Master Secretary Cecil had assured him that Henry Garnet had indeed been meddling in politics and, faced with this evidence, Gerard really should be sensible and give way.

"You cannot possibly know this", Gerard retorted, *"for you do not know the man. But I do and I know this to be false. He neither has nor would behave as you allege. Therefore I cannot do as you demand"*.

The Secretary of the Privy Council, again seeing he was to get no joy, turned on his heel and left the room.

Father Gerard was escorted back down to the torture chamber and had the manacles locked again most painfully onto his swollen hands. He was hoisted once more into the air, calling aloud to Our Lord and His Blessed Mother. For a long time he hung, conscious and praying, in unendurable pain until he fell, at last, into a coma. When, eventually, he revived, he discovered he was no longer hanging against the pillar but sitting, supported by persons round about. Someone had prised open his mouth and another was pouring warm water down his throat.

In charge now was Sir Richard Berkeley, the Lieutenant of the Tower, who asked whether it would not be better to submit to the queen's demands than to lose his life in this most horrible fashion?

"I repeat I cannot and I will not."

"Then we must hang you up again!"

"Let us go, then, in the name of God", Gerard answered defiantly, *for I would gladly die in this cause"*, and, for a third time, he was manacled

and the appalling barbarity was continued. But, after only an hour this time, the Lieutenant thought he had suffered enough and ordered the poor man back to his cell.

His gaoler actually wept at the pitiful sight of the tortured priest and did everything he could to help him. For three weeks Gerard could not move his fingers at all, not even to hold a knife and was thus unable to feed himself. But still his ordeal was not over for, a short time later, he was marched back down to the torture chamber to discover that he was about to be put to the rack. The torturers were standing ready, eager to get on with their bloodthirsty business. Terrified, and recalling to mind what had happened to his confrere, Edmund Campion, some years before, Gerard dropped to his knees and, in a loud voice, beseeched God to give him grace enough to endure the pain of being torn to pieces as He had given to the martyrs of old. He reaffirmed that come what may he would never betray Henry Garnet, his superior and an innocent man, even though they might literally rip his body apart upon their monstrous machine. Seeing that he was so resolute and mindful that they had been unable to force any submission from him before, the authorities relented and the courageous priest was returned, without further harm, to his prison.

By his indomitable spirit, Father Gerard seems to have won some regard from his brutal captors. Although still locked up in the Salt Tower, he was now left to his own devices, almost forgotten, it would appear, by the authorities. Although he was allowed no visitors, he was able to acquire a breviary and was allowed a bible. He made the Spiritual Exercises of St. Ignatius and practised the actions of the Mass in his cell. We can sympathise with this persecuted priest who had not been able to say Mass for so many months. He decided he must resume contact with his friends in the Clink and, to this end, he began to draw Bennet ever closer into his confidence.

Through his liking and sympathy for his prisoner, and with just a little pecuniary enticement, the warder was easily persuaded to run errands and letters to friends of the priest outside the Tower. But Bennet soon became anxious that it might be noticed that he spent so many hours away from his post and so Gerard arranged for his old friend, John Lillie, to be bought out of the Clink to run as an intermediary, and a bond of trust and understanding was soon established between him and the warder.

Huddington Court, Worcestershire

Chapter Five
Desperation and Frustration

During these months of confinement, however, Gerard's health began to decline through his weakened state. He needed fresh air and the Lieutenant was persuaded to give him permission to exercise on the wall adjoining his tower. This slight extra freedom was to bring dramatic and unexpected consequences for he became aware of another prisoner in a nearby tower taking similar exercise on the roof. This was John Arden, a gentleman from Northamptonshire who had been imprisoned for his faith and sentenced to death ten years earlier. The sentence had never been carried out and, during all this time, the only visitor had been his wife who brought him fresh clothes and other sundries he needed in a basket. She had always been such a regular caller that the warders had long ago ceased to check what she was bringing into her husband's prison and it suddenly occurred to Father Gerard that it might be feasible to say Mass in this gentleman's cell if he could only get him to understand what he meant and to ask his wife to bring in all the essentials for the Holy Sacrifice.

Father Gerard's round Salt Tower and the square Cradle Tower, in which Arden was kept, stood about forty yards apart on the south-east corner of the castle grounds and so oral contact was out of the question. After all, two men shouting to each other across the Queen's Privy Garden arranging for Mass to be said in the Tower of London might have attracted some sort of attention in 1597! So how to get his idea across? Perhaps Bennet could be persuaded to deliver a message, for he was Arden's gaoler also. After the initial refusal a little more money changed hands and Gerard's letter, which also concealed secret instructions written in orange juice which Arden could read when warmed over a fire, was delivered. Arden was enthusiastic and agreed to the scheme but proposed that after his wife had brought in all that was needed, Gerard should come over the same evening, stay the night and celebrate Mass early the following morning.

The proposal was sound but how to convince the warder to escort him to the Cradle Tower? This business was becoming dangerous. Obviously,

Gerard could not be allowed out of the Salt Tower on his own and, if they were challenged, it would have been all up for the warder as well. All Gerard's great persuasive skills were brought to bear upon the man who, at first, refused absolutely to cooperate in any way. What if the Lieutenant or any member of the Privy Council should take it into their heads to visit the priest that very day? What would become of himself if it became known that he had been so lax in his duty that he did not realise his prisoner was not in his cell? But Gerard reassured the worried man that this had never happened before and so he should put away his anxiety and receive, instead, a further bag of money!

"Aha, thank you, your worship. When did you say you would like to go across?".

"On September the eighth, the feast of the Nativity of Our Blessed Lady".

It was arranged accordingly that John Lillie should procure all the necessities and deliver them to Mistress Arden who would then bring them to the Tower in her familiar basket.

The plan was flawlessly executed. After everything had been arranged Father Gerard and Warder Bennet strolled nonchalantly across the Queen's Privy Garden to the other tower one evening, the turnkey whistling "Summer is a-cummin' in…" whilst keeping a furtive eye on the walls above! They were not observed.

And so it was that Father Gerard was at last able to say Mass for the first time in six months and we can only imagine the joy and encouragement that must have brought him. He describes it thus, *"The next morning, then, said I Mass, to my great consolation; and that great confessor of Christ (Arden) communicated, after having been so many years deprived of that favour. In this Mass I consecrated also two-and-twenty particles which I reserved in a pyx with a corporal; these I took back with me to my cell and, for many days, renewed the Divine Banquet with ever fresh and delighted consolation"*.

After Mass, the two men had breakfast and, as Arden's custom was, they climbed to the roof of the Cradle Tower to take the air. This tower was part of the southern curtain or outside wall of the castle's fortifications and Gerard, leaning over the battlements, was surprised to see that it rose directly from the moat. Although from his own prison built within the curtain walls he could just see the Thames through a narrow window slit, the priest had not expected to see the solid wharf which ran between the river and this moat, and an extraordinary thought sprang suddenly to mind which he voiced to Arden.

"Would it not be feasible to descend across the moat with the aid of a rope from this height?"

John Arden was startled and, taking in a gulp of air, he shot a doubtful glance over the drop towards the river; but he very quickly admitted that he was struck by the idea. "Yes, I believe it would!" he exclaimed. He warmed to the theme. "If we could fix one end up here and had some reliable friends on the other side who could attach the other end to the wharf it ought to be perfectly possible…with care! But there are guards on the wall and, even given a successful descent, how would we get away?"

"Leave that to me", answered Gerard with confidence. *"Such true friends I have who would certainly take the risk to rescue me; but, first, I must put the scheme to my superior to ascertain his mind".*

Through the good offices of his gaoler, Gerard was able to smuggle out an explanatory letter to John Lillie who delivered it to Father Garnet in his safe house within the city. The Superior was astonished and unsurprisingly dubious of a successful outcome to the daring proposal. Only a handful of prisoners had ever managed to abscond from the Tower of London in the five hundred years since its building by William the Conqueror, and Garnet was well aware of the fact. But, being conscious of the scarcity of priests on the English mission at the time, and of the continuing grave situation without his valued confrere, Father Garnet, more in hope than expectation, reluctantly approved the audacious attempt if Gerard himself considered the project practicable and prudent.

"Possibly not prudent, but I think we must try it!", was Gerard's response and he then appointed John Lillie and his former servant, Richard Fulwood, who was now in service with Father Garnet, to be the trusted agents, if they were willing, who would risk life and limb to secure the prisoners' clandestine release from the Tower.

Lillie and Fulwood were to row up the river at night with the help of any other reliable oarsmen they might need and secure their boat to the river side of the wharf. Gerard would then throw down to them one end of a length of twine attached to a ball of lead. These could be easily obtained by the warder. Lillie and Fulwood were to listen for the thud of this weight thrown over the moat and would tie the twine to the end of a rope they were to bring with them. Gerard and Arden would then haul up the rope and secure it to the cannon which stood permanently on top of the tower standing guard over the river. When the bottom end had been stretched and fastened to the wharf a quiet signal would be given and the descent of the two men could begin. That was the plan.

The idea was daring and exceptionally dangerous, but it was the only plan they had, and their only faint chance of escape.

On the appointed day of the proposed flight, Gerard prevailed upon the gaoler to allow him to visit his friend, John Arden, again. Being slightly more comfortable with the idea, since it had worked before, Bennet accepted the usual payment and favoured the request by escorting Gerard once more across the Queen's Privy Garden to the Cradle Tower; but he then locked the two men together in the cell before returning to the Salt Tower. Gerard and Arden had, therefore, to spend a great deal of time trying to loosen the stone into which the bolt was shot but, at last, they succeeded in emerging from the cell and reaching the top of the tower about midnight. They were just in time to see the boat approaching the wharf containing three men, Lillie, Fulwood and the helmsman from whom the boat had been procured. This man, unlikely though it seemed, turned out to be Gerard's former gaoler in the Clink!

Just as they were making fast to the wharf, a fisherman, clearly the worse for wear, staggered out of one of the small dwellings nearby to relieve himself in the river! Their amusement soon turned to consternation however as, seeing the men in the boat and taking them to be fishermen themselves, he engaged them in a hearty greeting. He soon retreated into his house, but the others felt they could not continue their business until they were certain the man was asleep and would not disturb them again. However, so much time had elapsed by then that they decided the rescue could not be accomplished before dawn and they made off back down the river.

Unfortunately, the tide was now so strong that it caught them unawares. They lost control of the boat and it became jammed fast against one of the many piers of the old London Bridge. For a long time they were in great fear of capsizing and drowning as the great force of water rushed wildly by; indeed, the helmsman himself was swept clean out of the boat and disappeared from view. But, after some time, a large sea-going vessel, manned by six sailors who had heard their cries, pulled out to rescue them. All this was witnessed with dismay and consternation by the men on the top of the tower as London Bridge, before its destruction in 1666, lay only a short distance away. Finally, they were greatly relieved to see the unfortunate last member of the crew being winched to safety onto the bridge.

The following morning Gerard was unsure of the changed situation. Perhaps the whole project should be abandoned as circumstances seemed now to suggest that the plan was doomed by being too ambitious and the outcome too unpredictable. God's providence, however, favoured the brave! John Lillie, who had so nearly drowned just a few hours before, sent a letter, via the warder, informing Gerard that, as far as they were concerned, nothing had changed, the plan remained intact and that he and the others would be returning that very night to bring it to a successful conclusion! This lifted Gerard's spirits mightily and he was able, with yet another small inducement, to gain the assent of the warder to allow him to stay a further day in the Cradle Tower.

It should be pointed out here that Gerard had been greatly concerned as to the fate of his gaoler who, although on the take, had also shown great kindness to him. But for this unwitting man, Gerard would not now have found himself in the position of making a possible escape from the Tower and so he had written three letters to justify his action. The first was addressed to Bennet himself explaining that he (Gerard) was *"but exercising my right, since I was detained in prison without any crime, and added that I would always remember him in my prayers."* This was to give the gaoler written proof to his superiors that he was not to be blamed for the break out. The second was addressed to the Lieutenant of the Tower further excusing the gaoler who knew nothing whatever of Gerard's plans and should, therefore, suffer nothing because of them. The third letter was addressed to the Lords of the Privy Council in which he set down the reason for his attempted bid for freedom. *"It was not so much for the mere love of freedom"*, he wrote, *"as for the love of souls which were daily perishing in England that led me to attempt the escape in order that I might assist in bringing them back from sin and heresy. Besides this, I exonerated the Lieutenant and gaoler from all assent to, or connivance at, my escape, assuring them that I had recovered my liberty entirely by my own and my friends' exertions".*

He then left all three letters to be discovered later in Arden's cell in the Cradle Tower.

Chapter Six
Escape and Devotion

Shortly after one o'clock in the morning Gerard and Arden crept
stealthily again to the top of the Cradle Tower and watched with bated
breath as the boat once more came silently to dock. Lillie and Fulwood
disembarked without mishap and Gerard hurled the twine, attached to its
lead weight, across the moat. This was safely retrieved and attached to the
rope which was then drawn up to the top of the tower and fastened to the
great cannon, placed there for its defence, and the signal was given from
below that all was prepared for the hazardous adventure to begin.

John Arden, on seeing the cable looping down and away into the
darkness, suddenly began to have second thoughts, but soon realised that
he had come too far for his courage to fail him now. He muttered a
fervent prayer and, with Gerard's blessing, and without further hesitation,
took life and rope into his hands and worked himself down, slowly but
surely, to the waiting men below.

John Gerard's descent was to prove much more difficult. Arden's weight
had stretched and slackened the thick and heavy rope and he was going to
have to labour much harder to propel himself along to a successful
landing. Added to this complication was the fact that his arms and hands
had not yet fully recovered from the terrible ordeal he had recently
endured in the torture chamber and so he could not grasp the cable as
strongly as he would have wished. He decided this might be less of a
problem if he were to let himself down backwards, legs first and facing
the ground, and so he clambered over the battlement and began the
perilous and painful journey down towards his anxious rescuers.

He had not travelled more than ten or twelve feet when he suddenly
slipped round under his own weight, and abruptly found himself swinging
underneath the sagging rope. The shock of this unexpected drop nearly
made him lose his grip altogether, but he managed to cling on and
readjust to the frightening new situation. This was precisely what he had
wanted to avoid. Gerard recalled, *"I could hardly get on at all. At length I
made shift to get on as far as the middle of the rope and there I stuck, my*

breath and my strength failing me, neither of which were very copious to begin with! After a little time, the saints assisting me and my good friends below drawing me to them by their prayers, I got on a little further and then stuck again, thinking I should never be able to accomplish it".

By now his arms were aching alarmingly and his hands, severely swollen again, were throbbing to the point of letting go. He even considered doing just that and taking his chances in the moat below; the landing would be such a relief, although uncomfortably damp, but the cool water would bring ease to his suffering limbs. However, he also realised that the impact of his drop would cause turbulence enough to rouse the castle. It would have meant his recapture and also the betrayal of his friends, who were already risking so much, and he therefore determined to summon, with an extraordinary last effort, whatever remained of his strength. He finally got so close to the other side of the moat that Lillie was able to grab his legs and so help to support him for the last few feet. Gerard was exhausted and unable to stand but he was somewhat revived by *"some cordial waters and restoratives…and, with the help of these, I was able to walk to the boat!"*

Quickly and furtively they scrambled in, shoved away from the wharf and breathlessly rowed some considerable distance before putting ashore to allow Arden and Lillie to slip away to a safe house which Gerard had been keeping, even during the time he had spent in prison. It had been looked after by Anne Line who had given shelter to many priests and Catholic laymen in London. This courageous lady was later hanged at Tyburn in 1601, after being convicted of, and proudly admitting to, harbouring Catholic priests.

Rowing on for a short distance Gerard and Fulwood then disembarked and soon reached another safe house where Gerard rejoiced to be reunited with his old friend, Nicholas Owen. He was waiting with horses ready saddled to further their journey hotfoot out of London to meet up with Father Garnet at White Webbs, his house in Enfield Chase, where a joyful thanksgiving was held in honour of this great deliverance. Father Gerard was able, at last, to lie low in safety while the frantic authorities turned London upside down in vain pursuit of the vanished priest.

This part of the adventure is not quite complete for we may be wondering what was happening back in the city and what fate would befall Gerard's gaoler. Gerard had prudently prepared a fourth letter, to be acted upon only if he got clear away. It was to be delivered to Bennet the following morning by Richard Fulwood, who caught up with him outside the Tower.

"Thank you", said the warder, taking the letter, "I will pass it on to him", thinking it was meant for Gerard
.

"No, no, not for the priest. This is for you, from a friend!"

"But I cannot read!" The confused man was becoming alarmed; no-one had sent him a letter before. "What is happening? What does it say?"

"You're not aware that Father Gerard and Master Arden escaped from the Tower last night? You are in the gravest danger. The Lieutenant has orders out and woe to you if you're taken! Do not go back to your post! Father Gerard has sent horses for your escape, your family too. We must leave immediately!"

The frightened man needed no second bidding and he, his wife and three children, as Gerard explains circumspectly, "...were spirited away to the house of a friend, one hundred miles distance from London". He does not specify which "friend" he meant but it is generally thought to have been Anne Vaux at Baddesley Clinton where Father Gerard and his confreres had been able to elude the priest hunters during the search of that house six years before, in 1591.

Gerard had therefore taken great care to see that Bennet and his family were well provided for and a year later he had the great joy of receiving his former gaoler into the Church! Bennet died five years after his conversion, "...having been through that trouble, rescued by God from the occasions of sin and, as I hope, brought to Heaven". Gerard continues, "My temporal escape then, I trust, was, by the sweet *disposition of God's merciful providence, the occasion of his eternal salvation".*

In the early hours of the fourth of October, 1597, Father John Gerard, S.J. accomplished a feat of resource and daring that not many had achieved before. By means of a stout rope and a few staunch friends he had broken out of the Tower of London and got clean away. As Catholic priests were really not allowed to escape from their Protestant captors, and especially not from the foremost fortress in the kingdom, this was actually against the law! A bit of a row erupted therefore when it was discovered that a hated Jesuit had unexpectedly and successfully challenged the savage might of the oppressive Elizabethan regime by the simple expedient of descending aerially from his prison and rowing away quietly in the middle of the night! This, obviously, was a typically shabby 'Catholick trick'!

Perhaps we should have some sympathy for Sir Richard Berkeley, the shaken Lieutenant of the Tower of London, who had to bear ultimate responsibility for this slight upon his custodial reputation. When he tried to explain to the Privy Council that he had the matter in hand as he had already sent out a posse to scour London for the miscreants, he was told by that august but exasperated body not to bother as he was wasting his time. "Do you not suppose, sir", they enquired angrily of the shame-faced Lieutenant, "that having planned and executed such an audacious thing, these unreliable subjects of Her Majesty would not also have had some regard for their own subsequent well-being outside our care and protection?"

That was it. The whole matter came to a conclusion within a few days and Father Gerard felt bold enough to emerge from hiding and resume his God-given mission.

So, having thus abruptly vacated his recent prestigious riverside address, Gerard set about procuring new headquarters in London. He decided that

42

the house in the charge of Anne Line would no longer be safe and so, in partnership with a Catholic supporter, he rented another property which contained a fine chapel. Now however, the authorities were offering a reward of one hundred pounds to anyone who would betray him and so, fearing that London really was now too unsafe, he soon retreated into the countryside to his old friends the Wisemans at Braddocks in Essex. But even here, because of his affection for the family and for the house that had so successfully concealed him three years before, he felt uneasy that he might yet be pursued and bring misfortune upon them all. And so, very reluctantly, he bade them farewell and, with Father Garnet's approval, accepted a long-standing invitation to take up residence as chaplain in the household of a Catholic lady in Northamptonshire.

That lady was Elizabeth Vaux, the grieving young widow of George, heir to the lordship of Harrowden. She was sister-in-law to Anne Vaux who had previously assisted Gerard and his superior along with five other priests to escape from the pursuivants at Baddesley Clinton six years earlier. Elizabeth now lived at the rather run-down Irthlingborough Hall which had belonged to her late husband. Even the usually polite Gerard described this building as being *"not only old, but antiquated!"*

The Vaux family seat was situated close-by at Great Harrowden but it, also, was in such dilapidated condition that Elizabeth was too embarrassed to lodge a priest in a house that would fail to provide decent shelter, let alone appropriate reception for the Catholic gentry who might come to visit him. Besides, there was no quick or secret bolthole from the place should it be approached by anyone with an inappropriate disposition towards a Catholic priest – and there were plenty looking for pay or advancements from the authorities in 1597.

But after much exploration Elizabeth and Father Gerard found Kirby Hall, a very large and rambling house built some twenty-five years previously in a remote and secluded part of the county which was deemed fit for their purposes, and a rent of one thousand, five hundred pounds was paid for a term of ten years – a vast sum in those days.

Soon after this, Father Gerard had to return to his London mission, and it was then that another treacherous servant struck. His testimony fell upon the itching ears of the Council and they sent the priest–hunters out to fall upon their unsuspecting prey.

They swooped suddenly at three o'clock in the afternoon against Gerard's new London address. There were a few others in the house to whom he was preaching a retreat and Gerard was himself at work on his priestly papers with his books open upon his desk when his servant, John Lillie, burst breathlessly into the room with his sword drawn. Explaining quickly that the pursuivants were already in the house, he advised the priest to take cover.

No sooner had Gerard taken off his soutane than the search party pounded up the stairs and pushed through the open door of the chapel opposite his room. They were thunderstruck, could not believe their good fortune. As Father wrote later, he recalled one of them exclaiming, "Good God! What have we found here?" There had been no time to clear the chapel and so the ruffians had discovered a huge haul of Mass equipment and the altar prepared for Mass with vestments already laid out by the side. It was, according to Gerard, *"all so handsome as to cause expressions of admiration, even from the heretics themselves!"*

While they were thus diverted, Gerard slipped out of his own room and, with the aid of John Lillie and the two ladies in the house, Anne Line and Mary Lady Lovell, Elizabeth Vaux's sister, he was able to gain access to a hide in the gable. He was unobserved but the enemy apprehended John Lillie whom they mistook for the priest. They had also by now found Father's books, papers and breviary for there had been no chance to spirit these away. Lillie quickly claimed them as his own so as to give no hint that the fugitive they had been pursuing since his escape from the Tower was even now sitting directly above their heads!

The villains were satisfied, however, that they had their man as he played the part with such great aplomb. Indeed, Gerard says, *" The ladies therefore, now perceiving that I was safe...and seeing John's assumed dignity, could scarce refrain from showing their joy...They wondered indeed and rejoiced and almost laughed to see him playing the Priest, for so well did he do it as to deceive those deceivers, and divert them from any further search".*

The mirth was short-lived however as the unfortunate John Lillie was carted off to the Tower of London and hung up in manacles just as his master had been tortured before. The inquisitors soon ascertained that the man they had apprehended was no priest at all, but they did discover that he had been instrumental in Gerard's escape. Naturally they wanted to know where Gerard was now, who were his friends and much more information of that kind, which Lillie absolutely refused to divulge even under the most extreme duress.

Seeing that further torture would have been useless he was transferred to Newgate to await execution. He met other Catholics there and, after a long imprisonment, contrived to escape with another priest. Father Gerard gives no further details, not even the name of the absconding cleric, no doubt for reasons of anonymity and security, as the method of decampment might still have been in use at the time of his writing in 1609.

After his escape John Lillie returned to his former master but they both recognised that he would now be a liability and, although he would have preferred to have kept him on as his servant and true friend, Gerard reluctantly put him under the protection of Father Garnet. From there Lillie travelled to Rome where, in 1602, he was admitted as a lay-brother into the Society of Jesus. Six years later he returned to England where he died of tuberculosis; *"...this truly faithful and prudent servant"*, remembered Gerard with great fondness and gratitude, *"was so full of charity as to offer his life for his friend. Truly his was an innocent soul and endowed with great prudence and cleverness."*

BROADOAKS IN ABOUT 1700.
(By courtesy of the Moravian Church, Fetter Lane, London.)

An early illustration of Braddocks, Essex

Chapter Seven
Hope and Disappointment

After his narrow escape in London John Gerard returned to Great
Harrowden, and preparations were set in hand for the anticipated move to
Kirby Hall. But, before any firm date could be established, it was decided
that a number of hides should be devised and constructed there and, to
this end, Father Garnet was happy to dispatch Nicholas Owen to
Northamptonshire along with another "partner in crime", Hugh Sheldon.

Nonetheless, rumours were already abroad that this huge mansion had
been taken with the express purpose of harbouring priests within its walls
and so, very early one morning, as Nicholas and Hugh were eating
breakfast before the day's work of constructing hides had begun, a raid
was made upon it in the hope of capturing the "well-known Jesuit, John
Gerard". But the priest had actually left for Irthlingborough the previous
evening and so the magistrate's party had to content themselves only with
the apprehension of Hugh Sheldon whom they interrogated to no avail
and later sent into exile. Nicholas Owen was fortunate that day and
slipped away, breakfast still in hand, through an unguarded door.

However, the priest-hunters had not quite finished their business for the
day. Acting upon information from spies set in the area they galloped off
after their quarry to Irthlingborough where they surprised the occupants at
dinner. Gerard had just enough time to snatch up a slice of bread and
meat, before rushing off into the hide already constructed there. Although
the house was searched thoroughly for the rest of the day, the hiding hole
had been so cleverly devised that nothing was found. Gerard gives no
clue in his writing as to what this refuge was nor where or how concealed
and so, alas, we shall never know its secret details as the building itself
has long since been demolished.

The frustrated pursuivants went home empty handed, but they had
actually achieved a small victory that day. Gerard writes, *"Those
Justices, who were pestilent heretics, and several others in the same
county, Puritans, declared they would never suffer her ladyship to live in
peace if she came there, as her only object was to harbour priests"*, and

so Elizabeth Vaux was forced to abandon all her plans for Kirby Hall; too much information about its intended purpose had already leaked out to the authorities. It was now far too risky to continue there, but another project had suddenly struck Elizabeth. Why should she not construct a secret addition to Great Harrowden to be used as a hidden base for these heroic priests?

And so it was done. Gerard continues, *"Here, then, she built a little wing of three stories (for us). The place was exceedingly convenient, and so free from observation that from our rooms we could step out into the private garden, and thence through spacious walks into the fields, where we could mount our horses and ride whither we would!"* In fact this wing fulfilled its design and was built so well that today it is the only part of the original building still standing.

There now followed a wonderfully long and uninterrupted period in which Father John Gerard's activities prospered and thrived. Using both Great Harrowden and London as bases he was able to journey out and meet many of the gentry of those parts in their own homes and in his. He was able to encourage, support and strengthen those who were beginning to tire in the fight for the Faith in the teeth of sustained and violent opposition from the Protestant authorities. He explained the Faith to those who knew little or nothing of it, and consoled those who, like himself, had been persecuted for it. He persuaded the doubtful, made converts of those seeking the true Faith of Christ and received many into the Church. He continued to arrange safe passage for young men to the Continent to try their vocations and, all the while, he was able to hear confessions, to celebrate Mass and to bring the great joy and comfort of Holy Communion to all those who adhered to the "Old Faith" (as it was referred to by now) despite the threat of fines, imprisonment and a barbarous death.

Ever present, of course, was the great fear of informers and the sudden, sickening thud on the door by the mailed fist of some keenly ambitious youth anxious to please his masters in the hope of some petty worldly advancement. Unfortunately, these zealots had no priest to explain to them that they were in danger of losing their own immortal souls, for they were hunting down, with hatred and iron, the very means of their eternal salvation. And so this era of unprecedented, murderous apostasy, this bloody Tudor century, drew depressingly to its dismal close and with it our "Good Queen Bess" fell slowly into mortal decline.

In order to live up to the image created by her sycophantic courtiers Queen Elizabeth I had long since taken to wearing an auburn wig. She also wore interesting amounts of make-up to disguise the blemishes left by a bout of smallpox in 1562 and to hold the ravages of time at bay to the point where Anthony Rivers, S.J., could write to Father Persons, "It was commonly observed this Christmas (1600) that Her Majesty, when she came to be seen at all, was continually painted, not only all over her face but her very neck and breast also, and that the same was in some places near half an inch thick!"

Perhaps she had come to believe the lie that if she looked young then obviously she would not be regarded as old, but soon the melancholy that had always been a part of Elizabeth's disposition came to dominate her whole spirit. She grew listless and began to grow anxious about her approaching end. More and more she became reliant upon her astrologer, John Dee, for advice both physical and spiritual (did this Supreme Head of the Church in England actually have any religion at all?), and early in 1603, he advised her to move from Whitehall to Richmond Palace where she would not have to keep up such a pretence of health and strength. It was here, after she had retired to her bed one night, that she had a terrifying dream of seeing herself asleep, her body emaciated and totally engulfed in a sea of flames. She woke up, petrified, and there now began a long period of insomnia during which she would not go to bed at all but would sit only on cushions all day and all night with a thumb in her mouth and a clammy dread of falling asleep in case the dream might be repeated.

Her dullness and lethargy greatly alarmed her ladies-in-waiting and those favourites who were allowed to visit. She once rebuked Admiral Lord Howard, who had encouraged her to return to her chamber to rest properly, by exclaiming, "You would not advise me of such a thing if you knew what I have seen. I cannot retire for I am tied with a chain of iron about my neck!" Once, in this state, she called for a mirror and, beholding a true reflection of herself minus the powder and the paint, received such a dreadful fright that she fell into an uncontrollable spasm, raging against all who had sought to flatter and deceive her. Reality had set in at last, but by now the Council had forbidden any word of the Queen's condition appearing on the streets - which was quite appropriate as the Queen herself had finally lost all power of speech!

With a frozen fear gripping her heart, Elizabeth I died on the 24th March, 1603, and almost before rigor mortis had set in, King James VI of Scotland who, from Edinburgh, had been keeping a keenly alert eye on the queen's deteriorating condition in London, having now received the gladsome tidings of her demise, was on his way south to add the English throne to his own.

With the dawning of the new Stuart Age, Catholic hopes were high and the Holy Father, Clement VIII, was pleased that the crown was passing, at last, from the excommunicated queen to a legitimate heir. The new king's mother had been the Catholic Mary Queen of Scots who, after nineteen years of imprisonment, had been beheaded in Fotheringhay on the order of her cousin, Elizabeth I in 1587. His wife, Anne of Denmark, was also a Catholic, at least on paper, and so it seemed reasonable to suppose with this history that James, rejoicing now in his collection of golden crowns, would be sympathetic to the Catholic cause and that better times would be on the way. It was confidently expected therefore that there would shortly be some abatement of Elizabeth's brutal laws for, whilst still in Scotland, James seems to have made promises of a conciliatory nature to various visiting English Catholics. For a short time, then, it appeared that this optimism would be justified as even John Gerard, writing in his memoirs later, noted *"...some hopeful signs of future favour"*.

However, to the great alarm of the Council, many people now expressed themselves to be of the old religion and Catholic numbers apparently grew rapidly. Was this because of new conversions or were there many closet Catholics who, with the coming of the new dynasty, now felt brave enough to declare themselves openly? Or might it even have been possible that the Council was exaggerating the numbers in order more easily to justify a heavier crackdown in the future? It is impossible to be certain, but what we do know is that there was to be no alleviation at all in the penalties against Catholics in these early months of James I.

Fines and imprisonment were as constant during this time as they had been under Elizabeth, due to the fact that Robert Cecil, Lord Salisbury, remained at his post of Chief Minister. Indeed, nothing had changed at all. All hopes of the lightening of the burden were irrevocably dashed upon the rock of a vitriolic speech made in Parliament by the new king in which he emphatically declared his "utter detestation" of the Catholic religion even though, quite unaccountably, he acknowledged it to be "the Mother Church of Christendom, but", he added, "there are many things in it which do not please me and so I do not embrace it." Given some of the king's known weaknesses, this was perhaps not to be wondered at! Finally, he declared that Catholics should not presume too much upon his leniency and should not consider it lawful for them "daily to increase their numbers and strength in my kingdom whereby they might be in hope to erect their religion again!"

Father Tesimond, S.J., a contemporary of John Gerard, relates in his 'Narrative of the Gunpowder Plot', "…James did more against us than Elizabeth had done in many years." For any gentleman of property, or of the merchant and commercial classes, non-attendance at the compulsory Protestant services had, under Elizabeth, meant a fine of twenty pounds per calendar month but, under James who listened to his vindictive ministers, this fine was increased to twenty pounds every four weeks. On top of this a brand new fine of ten pounds per month was proposed against his wife and children and the same yet again for his servants and household. Catholics began seriously to wonder, like Father Tesimond, "whether the little finger of the king was not now heavier than the shoulders of the queen?"

Even so, upon appeal to the king, Catholics were granted a reprieve before the actual confirmation of these harsh new proposals. They began to relax and, in gratitude for this possible revocation of more punitive legislation to come, praised the king for his mercy. This was probably just a touch optimistic as James then consulted three of his most trusted chums, Sir Edward Coke, the Attorney-General; Sir John Popham, the Lord Chief Justice and Sir Robert Cecil, Lord Salisbury, the Chief Minister of the Privy Council, who were the very architects of the original fines!

It did not come as any real surprise, then, that the cautiously growing optimism proved to be far from justified. Catholic hopes of a reprieve were finally confounded when the new levies were not only confirmed with greater vigour but were also to be back-dated to the death of the queen. Fines had to be paid instantly; there was to be no delay. All the oppressive anti-Catholic laws of Elizabeth I were hardened and the expulsion orders on the Jesuit priests, first issued in 1585, were now to be renewed with even greater energy - and all of this was to be accomplished within the lifetime of James' first Parliament. To make an example, Father William Weston, who had been a prisoner of Elizabeth for seventeen years, was deported to France from the Tower of London within twenty-four hours of the enactment of the harsh new decrees.

By comparison with what was to follow, his treatment was lenient, and Father Gerard and his confreres, well aware that so much worse was threatened, remained prudently in hiding, trying to come to terms with the possible barbaric death awaiting them if they were caught in the continuance of their God-given mission for the salvation of souls.

With the realization that all their hopes had been so savagely crushed and that life was to become even more grim and desolate under the new monarch, most Catholics groaned under this latest disappointment but recalled Our Lord's own words, "If any man will come after Me, let him deny himself, and take up his cross daily, and follow Me." (Luke 9:23). But some despaired of the intolerable new situation and, growing weary of the struggle and the strain on their already reduced purses, capitulated to the State in return for an easier life. And yet others, hot-headed and idealistic young men, a desperately motivated few, decided upon direct action against the State.

Chapter Eight
Gunpowder and Retribution

Robert Catesby, Thomas Wintour, John Wright, Robert Percy and Guy Fawkes, who liked to be known as Guido, were the instigators of what became known in their own time as the "Powder Conspiracy". Their ambitious plan was to blow up the Parliament House together with the king and the whole Privy Council, the lords, nobles and gentry in one almighty blast that would rid England forever of its ruling Protestant class. Nine other young idealists, many related, brothers, cousins or in-laws, were eventually brought into this bold design and the Gunpowder Plot was hatched.

Most Englishmen nowadays believe they know the infamous story behind the annual November 5th fireworks celebrations: how Guy Fawkes was caught in the act of lighting the fuse of an explosion that would have made the eruption of Krakatoa look like a garden bonfire, and hurrah! for the last-minute discovery by their great and clever king of a fiendish Popish plot!

This received version does not even begin to explain the convoluted story; it is much more intricate and puzzling than that – and much more exciting, too! Was it a Catholic plot? Was there a government infiltrator involved? Did the scheme become known to the authorities at the last minute, or halfway through its planning, or did they know about it from its very inception? Was it actually brewed by the malicious Cecil to implicate the priests and therefore prove that the Catholic Church was so deeply involved in politics that it would even connive at the assassination of a Protestant Head of State?

To be able to accuse the papacy of nefarious meddling in English governance and affairs of State, and therefore of treason against the monarch, was always the objective the anti-Catholic authorities had been pursuing for seventy hate-filled years. They had to find some justification for the guilt which must have haunted them for the destruction of English Christendom. They were desperate to find some excuse for the ongoing desecrations, murders, thefts and sacrileges begun by their grandfathers

53

under Henry VIII. They were therefore determined, by any means possible, to portray the Catholic priests as enemies and traitors to the peace of the kingdom. Perhaps then the blameworthy authorities, having found a scapegoat, would be able to enjoy more fully the dubious fruits of their unlawful inheritance.

The story of Gunpowder, Treason and Plot in English folk history is never old, and it will certainly be remembered. To the Catholic it is a mixture of both pride and shame: pride to imagine that some would be willing to risk their own lives in a foolhardy enterprise which might relieve Catholics of the burden of crippling fines and barbaric death; but, at the same time, shame that such an outrage could be contemplated in which so much innocent blood would also be spilled in trying to rid their country of the wicked oppressors. But to the Privy Council it was proof positive that Rome was not to be trusted and, to the conspiracy theorist of today, it provides a bottomless well that excites even the most febrile imagination. The gathering of the known facts and the many speculative conclusions that may be drawn into a definitive resolution of this intriguing episode in our history is yet to be done. Very likely, the whole truth will never come to light now; after all this time we can only guess at it.

Whichever way one looks at the reckless scheme, nothing went to plan. Whatever the truth of the story the actual result was exactly what Cecil had intended and was, therefore, devastating for John Gerard and the Catholic priests in England. Although they knew nothing about it and had nothing whatsoever to do with the Gunpowder Plot itself, the clergy were ultimately implicated in the affair by innuendo and the fiendish machinations of the Privy Council. Cecil recognised he had something meaty to get his claws into at last and was not about to let it go in a hurry. But, to relate here the whole history of the Gunpowder Plot would be to side-track the reader into a story of unnecessary length and detail; all we need to know is that Robert Catesby and his twelve associates had set in train a sequence of events that would have totally unforeseen and terrible consequences for Father Gerard and his confreres in England.

On the night of November 5th, 1605, all hell was let loose in London. Somehow, Guy Fawkes had been fortuitously arrested under the Parliament House, apparently in the act of setting light to a fuse that would have changed the course of English history. The frantic but jubilant government forces under Secretary Cecil burst out of ambush with orders to round up not only the actual conspirators but also any known Catholic, sympathiser or priest, who might have the least taint of treason brought against him.

No gunpowder had actually exploded anywhere - not even under the great and the good in Parliament as intended - but still the authorities reckoned their day had come! It was too good to be true and they now had all the excuse they needed to set out with vindictive glee to hunt down all those who could possibly have the least case made against them, which included individuals who, without proof, were only just suspected of holding the Catholic faith or of giving succour to the abhorred priests.

Guy Fawkes, giving his name upon arrest as John Johnson, held out against torture for two whole days. Salisbury then applied the one rack in the kingdom, the very same used to threaten Father Gerard, and eventually the beaten Fawkes, unaware of what he was doing, scrawled his signature, illegibly, upon a bogus confession he was certainly in no condition to read nor to understand.

The time gained by Fawkes' steadfastness under torture had enabled the panic-stricken conspirators to put some distance between themselves and the vengeful Cecil, but they were unaware that the authorities had already been alerted to be on the lookout for armed fugitives fleeing desperately through the Midland counties. Government spies were already watching many suspected Catholic houses situated in the wide band stretching from Essex westward to Worcester, so did Cecil therefore have prior knowledge of the Plot? Suspicions were certainly aroused at the time as the conspirators' trail was so quickly picked up.

The various parties, retreating via Warwick Castle and Coughton Court, gathered at Huddington Court on the night of 6th November. The following morning they heard Mass early and then set off in the pelting rain north into Staffordshire where the main group was cornered at Holbeach House. Here their leader, Robert Catesby, was shot dead along with three others. The rest of their companions were shot or otherwise wounded and taken prisoner. Over the next two months all the other conspirators were run to ground and captured. It was Robert Cecil, Lord Salisbury's greatest triumph.

However, although the prisoners were put to the torture and otherwise brutally treated, the authorities could extract no direct evidence from them that the priests had been in any way involved in the "Powder Treason" which should, indeed, have been ample evidence that they were not. Indeed, even Robert Cecil, Lord Salisbury, had later to admit that the plotters had not implicated the priests in any way, "...yea, what torture soever they were put to." But for now this was in no way to hinder the Council's main aim.

The hunt was now on. The Jesuits understood that the game was up and that all their heroic work in England must be abruptly terminated. They could not continue as before because their lives had been mortally endangered by the rash action of their co-religionists. All the anxious priests could do now was to slip fearfully into hiding and wait for the wrath of an avenging government to fall upon their heads. It was not long in coming.

Shortly after the discovery of the potentially Parliament-raising black powder in its vaults, the Northamptonshire pursuivants fell upon Harrowden Hall to detain Elizabeth Vaux and arrest any priest that might be found there. Father Gerard was actually in residence at the time but, being exceptionally adroit at self-preservation and knowing all the tricks by now, disappeared into a narrow hide where he could sit, but could not stand. He was cramped in there for a week while the hunting party poked, prodded and dismantled anything they fancied during the day and listened cunningly for any slight movement through the silence of the night. But, during times of supper for the search party, food was also taken secretly to him and once, during a night when the magistrate was distracted by other business, Gerard was carefully smuggled from his place of concealment and warmed by a fire.

Poor Elizabeth Vaux! How she must have yearned to show her guest better hospitality as she was forced to push the priest unceremoniously back into his place of restricted refuge! At one point, hoping to show the Justice that there was actually no-one in the house, she revealed the whereabouts of another hide. It was empty, of course, but it failed to persuade the man that the priest was not still hidden somewhere else close by. After nine days of fruitless probing and destruction the authorities gave up in frustrated rage. Thanks to Elizabeth's great courage and her selfless devotion and care, Father Gerard, confined to the small but ingenious hide, escaped detection yet again and so was able later to return safely to his London retreat.

In the meantime, Fathers Garnet and Oldcorne along with the two lay-brothers, Nicholas Owen and Ralph Ashley, who was servant to Father Oldcorne, had retreated to Hindlip House, the home of Thomas Habington near Worcester. It was an enormous building with a mass of elevated Elizabethan chimneys, lofty windows and vast roofs with a high tower surmounted by a stone cupola which commanded sweeping views over the countryside in all directions. But, most intriguingly of all, this astonishing place appears to have contained at least thirteen priest holes! It was as though the hides had been planned first and a far-sighted and devious architect had designed the rest of the house around them; and, as the structure had been built only thirty years after the Act of Supremacy, maybe it had indeed been so! The historian, Allan Fea, in his book, "Secret Chambers and Hiding Places" published in 1904, describes Hindlip thus: "In the quaint irregularities of the masonry free scope was given to (Nicholas Owen's) ingenuity… The walls of the mansion were literally riddled with secret chambers and passages. There was little fear of being run to earth with hidden exits everywhere. Wainscoting, solid brickwork or stone hearth were equally accommodating and would swallow up fugitives wholesale, and close over them, to "Open sesame!" again only at the hider's pleasure." It was into two of these hides that our four heroes now took cover as the local Justice suddenly appeared over the Worcestershire horizon.

After four terrifying days of listening to the alarming racket of bricks being smashed, panels splintered, glass shattered and floorboards clawed up all around them, Nicholas Owen and Ralph Ashley decided they could hold out no longer and took a chance on flight. They materialized from the woodwork in the library and quietly tiptoed through the door… straight into the arms of a surprised passing pursuivant! The pitiful men had eaten only one apple between them and were obviously starving but they may also have been anxious to distract attention from the priests who were still hidden somewhere in the house. If distraction had indeed been the ploy it didn't work for, although a number of hides had already been found, Mr. Justice Bromlie shrewdly reckoned there were probably more yet undiscovered; and he was pretty certain that the men the desperate Cecil really wanted, Fathers John Gerard and Henry Garnet, were surely almost within his grasp.

After several more days of destructive endeavour by the vandals, Fathers Garnet and Oldcorne, who had remained undetected throughout the search, could stand the strain no longer and suddenly emerged like phantoms from the fabric of the house. In fact they appeared so pale and exhausted that they literally looked like ghosts and the shocked men who came upon them so unexpectedly, at first turned tail in terror! Although there had been a little food in the hide there had been no room to stretch their aching bodies and numbed legs but, even more importantly, they had not had the convenience of an earth closet. Father Garnet opined later that had he and his companion been able to secure a commode they might have remained concealed for a month! They, too, were dragged off in chains to the Tower.

The eight surviving Gunpowder Plotters were tried at Westminster and all were hanged, drawn and quartered over two days; four in St. Paul's Churchyard and four in the Old Palace Yard, Westminster on the 30th and 31st January, 1606. They remained steadfast to the very end. None of them recanted their Catholicism and all exonerated the priests from having any part in their conspiracy.

Father Oldcorne, who had been Gerard's companion when they landed in the pouring rain on the Norfolk coast at the outset of their careers in 1588, and Ralph Ashley were hanged, drawn and quartered at Redhill near Worcester in April, 1606.

Nicholas Owen, who was suffering with a hernia, doubtless as a result of his heavy work in constructing priest-hides, was again hung up in manacles in the Tower and died the most barbaric death when his stomach, no longer able to withstand the extraordinary pressure, suddenly burst through his abdomen.

Father Garnet, after a shocking show-trial, was bound upside down on a hurdle and, with his head knocking against the cobblestones, was dragged off to St. Paul's to be hanged, drawn and quartered on May 3rd, 1606. But on the scaffold a sympathetic, though mainly Protestant, crowd surged forward to hang onto his legs in order to break his neck. Although this sounds cruel it was actually an act of mercy and was done to spare his being cut down while still alive and emasculated and disembowelled before his own eyes. Despite the fact that he was already dead, the authorities, not to be robbed of the usual entertainment, nonetheless ordered the prescribed bloody butchery be carried out on the block.

On the very same day, disguised as a servant in the entourage of an ambassador returning to Spain, Father John Gerard escaped out of England with the enraged Cecil, my lord the dignified Earl of Salisbury, still jumping up and down like a spoilt and frustrated child, screaming for his blood! Gerard always maintained that his safe deliverance was due to the intercession of his superior, the martyred Father Garnet.

Father John Gerard's exceptional eighteen fruitful years had, at last, run up against their unforeseen and abrupt end; but not before he had brought the comfort of Christ's own religion back to many of those who had almost come to the point of despair of ever again finding a priest who could forgive their sins, or of having the consolation of receiving Christ's true Body and Blood at the Holy Sacrifice of the Mass. At extreme cost to himself, Father Gerard, with God's own grace and authority will have saved a vast number of souls who would otherwise have been lost in the sustained murderous vision of the Protestant reformers.

Elizabeth Vaux continued her work of harbouring priests and was eventually arrested in 1611 when it came to the ears of the paranoid Salisbury that the slippery Father Gerard had returned to England! There was obviously no proof that the priest was hidden there, but Harrowden was ransacked yet again and Elizabeth condemned to Newgate prison when she once more refused to take the Oath of Allegiance. A year later she was released on the grounds of ill health and, carelessly defying all opposition, continued her great work for the Catholic faith until she died in 1625 at the age of sixty-one.

In actual fact, John Gerard was never able to return to the country of his birth but spent the remainder of his life relatively uneventfully in the service of Our Lord in Flanders, France and Italy. He wrote his autobiography at the behest of his superiors in 1609 and spent his last ten years as spiritual director of the English College in Rome where he died peacefully on July 27th, 1637.

He was seventy-three.

Let us pray, that all those who gave so much to aid Father Gerard and his kind in their heroic and dangerous labours for the Catholic Faith in those penal years, will have saved their own souls through the courageous work they facilitated, and may all the martyrs of England pray for us in our own times! Amen.

Michael Morley

Epilogue

There is a grand and fitting tribute to Father John Gerard's life and work in England, and it comes from a most surprising nineteenth century source. It was written by the Anglican Divine, Dr. Augustus Jessopp (1823-1914), a much-respected schoolmaster and clergyman in Norfolk and contributor to a Victorian edition of the Dictionary of National Biography. He wrote concerning Gerard in 1881:

"The extent of Gerard's influence was nothing less than marvellous. Country gentlemen meet him in the street and forthwith invite him to their houses; highborn ladies put themselves under his direction almost as unreservedly in temporal as in spiritual things. Scholars and courtiers run serious risks to hold interviews with him, the number of his converts of all ranks is legion; the very gaolers and turnkeys obey him; and in a state of society when treachery and venality were pervading all classes, he finds servants and agents who are ready to live and die for him.

"A man of gentle blood and gentle breeding – of commanding stature, great vigour of constitution, a master of three or four languages, with a rare gift of speech and an innate grace and courtliness of manner – he was fitted to shine in any society and to lead it.

"From boyhood he had been a keen sportsman, at home in the saddle, and a great proficient in all country sport. His powers of endurance of fatigue and pain were almost superhuman; he could remain in hiding days and nights in a hole in which he could not stand upright, and never sleep, and hardly change his position. He seems never to have forgotten a face or a name or an incident.

"Writing his autobiography twenty years after the circumstances he records, there is scarcely an event or a name which recent research has not proved to be absolutely correct. As a literary effort merely, the Life (Gerard's autobiography) is marvellous".

It would be difficult to find a more gracious summation of the life and adventures of this most brave of Roman Catholic priests.

Hindlip Hall, Worcestershire

Appendices

Beatifications:

Nine persons within this narrative are included in the list of the heroic faithful of those penal times, three of whom were beatified by Pope Leo VIII in 1886.

ALEXANDER BRIANT, S.J. - Hanged, drawn and quartered, Tyburn, 1581

EDMUND CAMPION, S.J. - Hanged, drawn and quartered, Tyburn, 1581

RALPH SHERWIN, S.J. - Hanged, drawn and quartered, Tyburn, 1581

The following six were beatified by Pope Pius XI in 1929.

HENRY WALPOLE, S.J. - Hanged, drawn and quartered, York, 1595

ROBERT SOUTHWEL, S.J. - Hanged, drawn and quartered, Tyburn, 1595

ANNE LINE - Hanged at Tyburn, 1601

NICHOLAS OWEN - Tortured to death, Tower of London, 1606

EDWARD OLDCORNE, S.J. - Hanged, drawn and quartered, Worcester, 1606

RALPH ASHLEY - Hanged, drawn and quartered, Worcester, 1606

———————————————————

Houses Mentioned in This Narrative:

BADDESLEY CLINTON, Warwickshire – National Trust, open to the public, 2 hides to view.

BROAD OAKS or BRADDOCKS, Essex – privately owned, contains John Gerard's most renowned hide under a fireplace, constructed by Nicholas Owen. (Illustrations on pages 46 and 73.)

COUGHTON COURT, Warwickshire – jointly owned by the National Trust and the Throckmorton family, open to the public, 3 hides to view.

GREAT HARROWDEN, Northamptonshire – demolished in 1721, a privately-owned Georgian house now stands on the site.

HINDLIP HALL, Worcestershire – demolished in 1814 after a fire. The cellars survive but are unavailable to view as the present building on site is West Mercia Police HQ! However, the site itself is still worth a visit; with permission you may check out the surrounding vistas and the original church nearby - and imagination will do the rest. (Illustration on page 62.)

HOLBEACH HOUSE, Staffordshire – privately owned, still contains 2 original hides although the earlier Elizabethan building was largely, but not completely, destroyed by the fire started at the time of Catesby's death; the present house is mostly Jacobean.

HUDDINGTON COURT, Worcestershire – privately owned, contains 2 hides constructed by Nicholas Owen. (Illustrations on pages v. and 32.)

IRTHLINGBOROUGH HALL, Northamptonshire – long ago demolished or fallen down.

KIRBY HALL, Northamptonshire – National Trust, open to the public.

TOWER OF LONDON – The Salt Tower (John Gerard's prison) and Cradle Tower (John Arden's prison from which the escape was made) are open to the public. (Illustration on page 10)

WHITE WEBBS, Enfield Chase – exact site uncertain but long since demolished, (a pity, for apparently it rivalled Hindlip Hall in the labyrinth of hides constructed there).

N.B. HARVINGTON HALL, Worcestershire, (which does NOT feature in the narrative), contains by far the best series of priest holes of any house in England today. There are eight hides in total, six of which can be easily seen. It is owned by the Catholic Archdiocese of Birmingham and is open to the public. Harvington Hall is highly recommended as it gives a very clear idea of the nature of some of these carefully constructed and ingeniously sited hides. Very well worth a visit!

There are very many other houses around the country which contain priest holes. A good number of them are readily accessible as they are owned by the National Trust or English Heritage. Check them out!

Privately owned houses will, naturally, need permission from the owners to view their hides.

The Papal Bull 'Quo Primum'

The years of "reformation" since 1517 when Martin Luther posted up his Thirty-nine Articles, had caused chaos within the (Catholic) Church to the point where people were facing all kinds of different versions of the Mass throughout Europe. The faithful could no longer be sure which service was legitimate and which was not; which priest was holding to tradition and which had accepted the new Protestant theology which would have made the Mass invalid. The confusion amongst the faithful was therefore immense and widespread.

The issue was further complicated by the fact that before the Reformation there had been many recognised true and legitimate rites of Mass throughout Europe; e.g. in England there were various rites celebrated in York, London, Hereford, Sarum (old Salisbury) etc. according to each diocese, although transubstantiation (the changing of the bread and wine into the true Body and Blood of Christ) at the canon or heart of the Holy Sacrifice had, of course, remained the whole raison d'etre of all the diverse liturgical celebrations.

Faced with this tumult, Pope Pius V was determined to settle peace upon the Church now being attacked by many forms of heresy which were disturbing the Rock of Peter. Thus, as the most important part of the Counter-Reformation, and at the request of the Council of Trent, he issued the papal bull "Quo Primum", so-called from the first two Latin words of the decree. This proclamation, introduced with all the force of his apostolic authority, commanded that the Latin Rite of Mass, then pertaining in Rome should, by law, henceforth and forever be the liturgical norm to be celebrated throughout the whole Catholic world.

This form, promulgated in July, 1570, came to be known popularly as the "Tridentine Mass" and the bull ended with the dire warning that if anyone in the future should dare to alter this decree in any way, ".... he should know that he will incur the wrath of Almighty God and of the Blessed Apostles Peter and Paul." But having great solicitude for the equilibrium of his flock, the Holy Father also declared for the sake of continuity and their comfort, that any pre-existing rite with a continuous usage of at least two hundred years before this date should be allowed, if the local bishop thought it expedient, to continue for a time until it could be gradually replaced by his revised Roman Missal of 1570.

The Canonical Hours

The monastic community was perfectly ordered, and all its members were obliged to live by a strict timetable of prayers known as the **Horarium**. This was governed by the eight canonical hours, each announced by the ringing of a bell and set three hours apart, so making up the twenty-four hour day.

They were as follows:

1. 12 Midnight   **Matins**
2. 3 am   **Lauds**
3. 6 am   **Prime**
4. 9 am   **Terce**
5. 12 Noon   **Sext**
6. 3 pm   **None**
7. 6 pm   **Vespers**
8. 9 pm   **Compline**

….and so start again at midnight the following day.

Selected Bibliography

Camm, Dom B., Forgotten Shrines, 1910

Caraman, P., S.J., (Transl.), John Gerard: The Autobiography of an
      Elizabethan, 1951

Cobbett, W., A History of the Protestant Reformation, publ. 1824-27.
      (Ed. H. Arnold, 1994). This is a <u>very highly recommended</u>
      history of the Reformation from a non-Catholic point of
      view; from the author of 'Rural Rides'.

Durst, P., Intended Treason, 1970

Edwards, F., S.J., Guy Fawkes, 1969

Fea, A., Secret Chambers and Hiding Places, 1904

Fraser, A., The Gunpowder Plot: Terror and Faith in 1605, 1996

Hodgetts, M., Secret Hiding-Places, 1989

Hodgetts, M., A Topographical Index of Hiding Places, Recusant
      History, Catholic Record Society, 1982

Hogge, A., God's Secret Agents, 2005

Lunn, D., The Catholic Elizabethans, 1998
Morey, A., The Catholic Subjects of Elizabeth I, 1978

Morris, J. (Ed.), S.J., The Condition of Catholics Under James I, 1871

Morris, J. (Ed.), S.J., The Troubles of our Catholic Forefathers, 3 series,
        1872

Reynolds, T., St. Nicholas Owen, Priest-Hole Maker, 2014

Squiers, G., Secret Hiding-Places, 1934

Tesimond, O., S.J., The Narrative of the Gunpowder Plot, ca.1608
        (Reprint ed. F. Edwards, S.J., 1973)

Thurston, H., S.J., The Gunpowder Plot, Catholic Truth Society, 1929

Waugh, M., Blessed Nicholas Owen: Jesuit Brother and Maker of
        Hiding Holes, Catholic Truth Society, 1961

The Hide at Braddocks

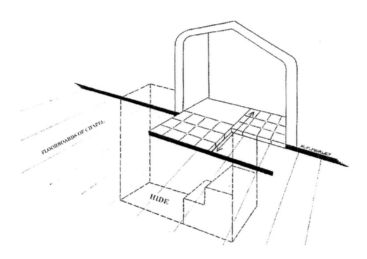

FLOORBOARDS OF CHAPEL

HIDE

M.F. MORLEY

Index